"Michelle Dudash comes 'clean' with the best ways to feed families hungry for healthy, kid-friendly foods. Now if we could just get them to clean the dishes!"

—Carolyn O'Neil, M.S., R.D., co-author of *The Dish on Eating Healthy and Being Fabulous!* and "Lady of the Refrigerator" on Food Network's *Good Eats*

"Michelle Dudash displays a passion for delicious food that's easy to make and good for you, too. She simplifies how to feed your family healthy meals, snacks, and side dishes without sacrificing great taste. As a mother of three, I really appreciate that!"

—Elizabeth M. Ward, M.S., R.D., author of *MyPlate for Moms: How to Feed Yourself & Your Family Better*

"Michelle's practical tips will easily enable any on-the-go mom or dad to prepare healthy and delicious recipes for their families while embracing the concept of local and sustainable food. The scrumptious recipes and gorgeous food photography speak for themselves."

—Toby Amidor, M.S., R.D., C.D.N., nutritionist and blogger for FoodNetwork.com's Healthy Eats blog

"What a refreshing alternative to take-out! This is 'fast food' that parents can feel good about."

—Denise Maher, health and nutrition editor and founder of Alternahealthgrrrl.com

CLEAN EATING
FOR **BUSY** FAMILIES

Get Meals on the Table in Minutes with

Simple & Satisfying Whole-Foods Recipes

You & Your Kids Will Love

MICHELLE DUDASH, R.D.

First published in the USA in 2012 by
Fair Winds Press, a member of
Quayside Publishing Group
100 Cummings Center
Suite 406-L
Beverly, MA 01915-6101
www.fairwindspress.com

16 15 14 13   3 4 5

ISBN: 978-1-59233-514-5

Digital edition published in 2012
eISBN: 978-1-61058-622-1

Library of Congress Cataloging-in-Publication Data available

Book and cover design by Rita Sowins / Sowins Design
Photography by Nutrition Studio (http://nutritionstudio.com)
Author's hair and makeup by Diane Aiello

Printed and bound in China

The information in this book is for educational purposes only. It is not intended to replace the advice of a physician
or medical practitioner. Please see your health care provider before beginning any new health program.

TO MY HUSBAND, STEVE, FOR HIS ENDLESS SUPPORT AS I PURSUE MY DREAMS.

TO DARLING SCARLET—FOR WITHOUT HER, THIS BOOK WOULD NEVER HAVE COME TO BE.

CONTENTS

CHAPTER 1

CLEAN KITCHEN KNOW-HOW

KNOW-HOW

GETTING STARTED, SHOPPING LISTS & TIPS

"MY BIGGEST PROBLEM IN THE KITCHEN IS COMING UP WITH NEW DINNER IDEAS THAT ARE HEALTHY, TOO; DISHES THAT ARE EASY TO MAKE, NOT WEIRD, AND DON'T FORCE ME TO GO TO THREE DIFFERENT STORES TO FIND THE INGREDIENTS. I FEEL LIKE WE EAT THE SAME THING EVERY WEEK. TAKEOUT IS EASY, BUT IT'S FATTENING. WHAT DO YOU MAKE FOR DINNER? DO YOU HAVE ANY RECIPES FOR ME? HELP!"
— Busy Moms Everywhere

Does that sound familiar? It's typically the beginning of most of the conversations I have with the many moms I talk to. Whether from television host coworkers, attendees at speaking engagements, or stay-at-home moms at cocktail parties, it's one of the questions I'm asked most frequently, as soon as people find out I'm a chef and registered dietitian.

The reality of cooking for my family hit home for me after the birth of my baby Scarlet. For several days straight even I, the chef nutritionist, stared into the refrigerator wondering what I'd have time to make for dinner. On one such occasion I figured out how to adapt my lighter chicken curry recipe to the slow cooker, and that's when the idea for this book hit me. Over the next few months I created original and improved recipes that fit my new-mom lifestyle. Just like moms often choose a shorter hairstyle and more practical shoes, I adopted a simpler, easier style of cooking using clean ingredients. Now I want to inspire and educate other families about how easily they, too, can eat clean with a little knowledge.

{ My Five Food Rules for Eating Clean }

The clean concept boils down to eating whole, minimally processed foods made with natural ingredients that are good for your body and good for the planet. Keep these tips in mind, and you'll be on your way in no time:

1. CHOOSE FOODS CLOSEST TO THEIR NATURAL STATE

The less processed foods are, the more naturally occurring vital nutrients and the fewer harmful ingredients they contain. Also, if you can't pronounce an ingredient on the label, you probably shouldn't eat it. Instead of components that sound like things from lab experiments, opt for foods with ingredients you find in home kitchens.

Especially avoid these ingredients:

» Partially hydrogenated oil
» Artificial food coloring (Blue 2, Green 3, Red 3, Yellow 5 and 6)
» Artificial sweeteners (acesulfame potassium, saccharin, aspartame)
» Nitrates and nitrites in cured meats
» Large amounts of refined added sugars and salt

2. ENJOY A COLORFUL ARRAY OF FOODS

Each color of the rainbow provides a unique blend of disease-fighting, immunity-boosting antioxidants, phytochemicals, vitamins, and minerals. The more natural colors you choose, the more varied and inclusive your diet will be.

3. GO LOCAL AND SEASONAL

Foods that travel shorter distances to get from farm to fork leave a smaller carbon footprint, making them better for the planet. The closer, the better, but find what is comfortable for you. Start by reading the signs next to your produce and the labels on the backs of packages. Ideally, choose foods from your country rather than the other side of the world. Even better, choose foods from within your region, state, or county. This doesn't have to mean making multiple trips to farmers' markets if they are more than a few minutes away.

Most foods taste better and contain higher amounts of nutrients when they're eaten during peak season and haven't been sitting in warehouses for months. Dried foods and foods frozen or canned within days of harvest come in at a close second. The better foods taste naturally, the less you have to manipulate them with added sugar, fat, and salt.

4. CHOOSE HUMANELY PRODUCED FOODS THAT ARE GOOD FOR THE PLANET

Learn what you can about the companies you buy food from. Do the farmers treat their animals well? Are the plants sprayed with minimal amounts of pesticides or, preferably, none? How do the companies treat their employees, and what is their regard for sustainable practices? While you probably won't find all of these answers on the backs of food packaging, glean what you can from company websites and the media. Every time you check out at the grocery store, you are voting for who will fail or succeed.

5. ENJOY EVERY BITE

Food not only nourishes and fuels our bodies and minds, it also provides entertainment, encourages curiosity, invites togetherness, and rejuvenates the soul. Food should taste good first and then be good for us also. A variety of flavors, including salty, sweet, sour, pungent, and bitter, paired with different textures, makes for the most satisfying meal. We should feel free to savor flavorful foods until satisfied, rather than eat around cravings and long for something else minutes later. As often as possible, enjoy food intentionally while seated at the table and avoid mindless snacking.

{ Getting Started Right Away }

I've structured this book so that you can start cooking clean immediately, with this introductory chapter providing helpful, but not essential, background information. I've also sprinkled "Go Green" and "Go Clean" sidebars throughout the recipes, enabling you to learn along the way as you cook. "Go Green" sidebars focus on local and seasonal eating tips, while "Go Clean" sidebars focus on eco-friendly practices and nutritional tips.

I'm a busy mom, too, with a crazy, active toddler and somewhat choosy husband whom I cook for in between balancing my business and household. I get to the gym and enjoy a bit of social time on the weekends. In other words, I'm not slaving over the stove for hours and washing piles of dishes each day.

WHAT YOU'LL LOVE ABOUT THESE RECIPES

Easy-to-Find Ingredients: You should be able to find all of the recipe ingredients in mainstream grocery stores, saving you the time of searching at multiple specialty markets.

Mom Tested, Family Approved: I tested all of these recipes on my family and on my "mommy" consumer panel. Recipes appeal to kids and adults alike, decreasing your chances of having to cook two different menus for one meal.

Fast and Efficient: Most recipes take only thirty minutes or less of active prep time, saving you time in the kitchen. You'll see these recipes marked with a **< 30** icon. As much as possible, my recipes call for quantities using entire units of perishable foods, leaving you with one less thing to wrap, put away, and worry about using up before the expiration date.

Centered on Dinner: The number one request I receive from moms is for evening meal ideas. I am responding by featuring mostly main dishes. I've added starters, sides, and desserts, for when you want (or need!) to go the extra mile for guests, parties, and potlucks.

One-Dish Meals: I include vegetables in main dishes whenever possible, hoping to streamline dinnertime. Vegetables replace a portion of the meat to help keep calories in check, boost nutrients, and protect the planet.

Satisfying, Yet Calorie Conscious: Adding vegetables to most dishes allows for larger portion sizes with only a few more calories, keeping you fuller longer. I use the perfect balance, never an excess, of healthy fats and salty ingredients to make each dish sing. Each recipe includes a nutritional analysis.

Substitutions at Your Fingertips: I offer substitutions within recipes for fresh herbs and other ingredients that you might not have on hand.

Seasonal Substitutions: I offer alternative ideas for produce in peak season year-round.

A Variety of Methods to Suit Your Preferences: You'll find quick stovetop techniques, "fix-it-fast and cook-it-low" slow-cooker dishes, and make-ahead-and-bake casseroles. I also include recipes for grilling to reduce the number of dirty pans. And speaking of pans, I'm mindful of keeping the required number of pans and dishes to a minimum to allow for faster cleanup.

{ Yes, You Can Do This }

If you picked up this book, I'll bet you're a great parent. You want to feed your family well and make good decisions. But I know the questions going through your head. "My schedule is so packed; do I have time to cook?" "Will my family eat healthy foods?" "Can I afford it?" Ordering takeout, going to get it, and cleaning up afterward can take just as much time and money—if not more—as preparing a delicious home-cooked meal. Learning to eat healthier is a gradual process. Instead of thinking all or nothing and cutting out everything you love, focus on specific changes you are willing to make and stick to. Maybe you'll start by incorporating more vegetables into your meal planning. Or perhaps switching to brown rice would be an easier adjustment. You don't have to go "cold turkey." Start with what's realistic and build on it.

{ Getting Your Family on Board }

You like it better when you are *asked* to do something rather than told, right? While planning meals, you might start by asking your family, "Chicken or fish tonight?" "Italian or Mexican?" "Pasta or rice?" When people feel empowered to make decisions, they will be more likely to embrace change. Bring your child to the market with you on a good day and invite him to pick out a vegetable. If you have a particularly picky eater, consider trying some of the tips in the following sidebar.

{ Shopping Tips and Tricks }

The better stocked your kitchen is, the easier it will be to eat clean with minimal time and effort. I'll admit that I'm not the perfect meal planner. My husband's and my tastes change from day to day, and we don't know exactly what we'll be in the mood for. Sometimes I lack inspiration until I spot a beautiful piece of fresh produce at the store. I rely on a well-stocked pantry and fridge for the peace of mind that I have an arsenal of staples on hand to accompany whatever fresh ingredients I buy.

Following are some of my tips for what shopping to do when and how to divide up your grocery lists. With a basic plan in place, you can pull together meals at a moment's notice.

TEN TIPS FOR DEALING WITH PICKY EATERS

I did all the "right" things while my daughter Scarlet was a baby: breastfed, made homemade baby foods in a variety of unconventional flavors, and puréed adult meals that she gobbled up. Then she turned two and became much choosier. Some tricks that help overcome pickiness follow.

1. **Don't Give Up.** Continue to offer, not force, a variety of foods, namely vegetables, with most meals. It can take eight to ten exposures before a child decides whether she likes a new food or will even try it! Eventually, your child will probably surprise you.

2. **Make Snacks Count.** As much as your child may beg for butter crackers, offer him nutritious foods such as grapes and cheese. At least if he doesn't eat his dinner, you know he received nutritious food prior.

3. **Offer Fruit at Every Meal.** That's one healthy food most kids will eat.

4. **"Healthify" Favorites.** If she loves fast-food chicken nuggets, try my baked salmon nuggets (page 60). The crunchy crust fooled Scarlet!

5. **Offer Vegetables First.** The period prior to dinner is an excellent time to break out the vegetable snack sticks and dip. If he is hungry, serve it and he will come.

6. **Pair It with a Dip.** Everyone loves to dip. Pairing a new food with your child's favorite dip may serve as the bridge to get him to eat the foreign food.

7. **Have Whisk, Will Try It.** Involving your child in the cooking process will increase the chances of her eating healthier. At age two, a child can start adding and stirring ingredients. Scarlet wouldn't eat pancakes until the day she got to pour the ingredients into the bowl and mix the batter. Now she begs me to make whole-grain pancakes with her. Even allowing a child to sprinkle cheese over a dish for a finishing touch will give her a sense of empowerment.

8. **Size Matters.** Shredding, dicing, slicing, and puréeing vegetables into a child's favorite foods are excellent ways to get his palate accustomed to new flavors.

9. **Keep the Junk out of the Trunk.** Save the "unclean" treats for special occasions, if you must serve them at all. If it's not in the house, your child can't torment you with incessant begging.

10. **Be a Positive Role Model.** Since a child mirrors the actions of role models (that's you) in her life, I can't stress enough how important it is to make healthy choices in front of your child. Guess what Scarlet's favorite snack is (besides mini cheese crackers, of course): pistachios! And she devours hummus, a favorite afternoon snack of mine. "Programming" your child's taste buds and preferences early sets the stage for a lifetime of good eating habits.

WEEKLY SHOPPING

Make quick weekly sweeps through the market for fresh proteins, produce, dairy, deli, and baked goods. If you know you'll be eating dinner at home three nights this week, you can decide on three recipes you will prepare or three proteins and vegetables.

SUGGESTED WEEKLY SHOPPING LIST

» Snack vegetables, such as baby carrots, celery, sugar snap peas, jicama, and cherry tomatoes
» Dinner vegetables
» Seasonal sandwich and salad vegetables: tomatoes, avocados, and cucumbers
» Lettuce greens
» Italian flat-leaf parsley
» Scallions
» Fruit: berries and stone fruit (spring, summer), apples, grapes, and pears (fall), and citrus and kiwi (winter)
» Dairy or nondairy substitutes: low-fat Greek yogurt, milk, cottage cheese, kefir, and shredded, sliced, and snack cheeses
» Baked goods: 100 percent whole-grain (sprouted preferred) sliced bread, English muffins, and tortillas
» Hummus dip
» Vegetarian-fed eggs
» Fresh tofu and tempeh
» Seafood, such as tilapia, salmon, barramundi, shrimp, rainbow trout, and cod
» Poultry, mostly skinless
» Lean meat, such as pork tenderloin and chops; bison; and organic or grass-fed ground beef, or flank steak

BUSY FAMILY CONVENIENCE FOODS

Following are a few smart choices for packaged foods, should your family find them helpful to have on hand:

» Lower sodium soups and canned vegetables
» Fruit cups in 100 percent fruit juice or water
» Lower sodium natural deli meats
» Natural granola or snack bars with fruit, nuts, or whole grains listed as the first ingredient
» Whole-grain tortilla chips made with nutritious oils
» Natural microwave popcorn

MONTHLY SHOPPING

Set aside a couple of hours to shop each month without the kids. Shop with a plan and stock up on grains, frozen and canned goods, and other staples. I recommend keeping a running list on the fridge so that when you are tasked with writing the list you already have a head start and won't forget to restock when you run low.

SUGGESTED MONTHLY SHOPPING LIST

» Produce for recipes: lemons and limes, yellow onions, celery, carrots, potatoes, and garlic
» Frozen peas, corn, carrots, and shelled edamame
» Variety of whole-grain rice, pasta, and quinoa
» 100 percent whole-grain breakfast cereal and granola
» 100 percent whole-grain crackers
» Brown rice cakes
» Salad dressing made with olive or canola oil and minimal added sugar
» Tub spreads made with olive or canola oil and no hydrogenated oils
» Nuts and seeds
» All-natural nut and seed butters with no hydrogenated oils
» Dried fruit with minimal or no added sugar
» Organic or reduced sodium broth (vegetable, chicken, and beef)
» Pouches of salmon and light tuna
» Canned or dried beans: garbanzo, black, white, kidney, and pinto
» Cans or cartons of tomato products: whole, diced, crushed, sauce, and paste
» 100 percent fresh fruit juice
» Treats if you choose: dark chocolate, natural whole-grain cookies, dark-chocolate-dipped fruit and nuts

QUARTERLY SHOPPING

These foods last awhile when stored properly, so buy the right amount that will see you through a few months and streamline the shopping process.

SUGGESTED QUARTERLY SHOPPING LIST

» Oils: cold-pressed extra-virgin olive, expeller-pressed canola or grapeseed, dark sesame, and corn
» Vinegars: balsamic, apple cider, white distilled, rice, red wine, white wine, and sherry
» Cooking oil spray (chlorofluorocarbon-free): expeller-pressed canola and olive oil
» Dried herbs and spices
» Nutritional yeast seasoning (adds umami [savory] flavor to meatless dishes)
» Condiments: olive oil or canola mayonnaise, natural ketchup, and tamari or reduced sodium soy sauce or liquid amino acid concentrate
» Tea leaves or tea bags
» 100 percent whole-grain flour
» Pasta sauce made with extra-virgin olive oil
» Thick-cut oats
» Flaxseed meal
» Sweeteners: honey (not for babies younger than one year), evaporated cane juice, agave nectar, real maple syrup, stevia, and molasses
» Low-processed sea salt

{ My Favorite Busy-Family Tools }

While many of these kitchen tools aren't absolutely necessary, they will cut your time in the kitchen and enhance your cooking experience.

» Good-quality, 12-inch (30 cm) frying pan with ovenproof handle (the workhorse of the busy family)
» Good-quality, 12-inch (30 cm) skillet (straight-sided) with ovenproof handle
» Good, sharp knives: vegetable (Santoku), fish, boning, and paring
» Microplane grater: use for citrus zest, Parmesan cheese, and nutmeg
» Kitchen shears
» Food processor: a small one for most jobs and a large one for big jobs
» Small, medium, and large cutting boards
» Lemon and lime presses or reamer

- » Fish spatula for handling delicate fillets
- » Spider skimmer for lifting vegetables and pasta out of water
- » Wooden spoons with rounded and flat edges
- » Heatproof silicone spatulas and scrapers
- » Good pepper mill (I always use freshly ground pepper instead of the bottled dusty stuff.)
- » Silicone steamer basket insert with lid
- » Parchment paper and silicone baking mat for easy pan cleanup
- » Salad spinner for washing, draining, and drying fruits, vegetables, and herbs
- » Grill basket

{ A Few Final Cooking Tips }

Take a minute to quickly run through these final tips to ensure cooking success.

Check Your Oven Temperature: Especially if you have an older oven, it is a good idea to test its accuracy from time to time with an oven thermometer. It is not uncommon to find ovens that vary twenty-five to fifty degrees from their target.

Measure Prepared Ingredients Properly: If the ingredient prep instructions are listed after the comma (i.e. 1 cup [144 grams] strawberries, chopped), measure the ingredient first and then prepare as described. If the ingredient prep instructions are listed before the comma, or if there is no comma, (i.e. 1 cup [144 grams] chopped strawberries), prep the ingredient first and then measure.

Measure Dry Baking Ingredients Properly: Pour or spoon flour and cocoa into a dry measuring cup and then scrape a flat knife across the top for a level measure.

Use a Hot Pan and Hot Oil: For maximum flavor, add oil to a hot pan, and food to hot oil, unless otherwise specified.

Opt for Hot and Heavy Pans: I use heavy-bottomed stainless steel pots and pans, which can get hotter than lightweight pans. I also cook on an electric stove at home. Adjust cooking times and temperatures accordingly based on the equipment you use at home.

{ All Aboard the Clean Eating Train! }

With a well-stocked kitchen, a little planning, and a willingness to try a few new tricks, eating clean can be accomplished with little time and effort. Making the switch doesn't have to be all-or-nothing, and with every change, each day, week, and month, you and your family will be eating healthier with every bite.

CHAPTER 2

SATISFYING SALADS, SOUPS & APPETIZERS

RED POTATO SALAD WITH SCALLIONS & GREEK YOGURT

Scarlet devoured deli potato salad until I decided to upgrade to a homemade version without the additives. The eggs add protein, making this nearly a meal in itself for a ravenous child. For the very choosy eaters who pick the vegetables out of dishes, try cooking the celery with the potatoes to give it a soft texture and muted color that blends right in. Linda, a recipe tester and fellow registered dietitian, served this potato salad at a party and loved that it didn't taste at all like a "light" recipe.

4 cups (440 g) ½-inch (12 mm) cubed
   red potatoes
½ cup (115 g) light mayonnaise
½ cup (115 g) nonfat plain Greek yogurt
2 teaspoons (10 g) dill pickle relish
2 teaspoons (8 g) Dijon mustard
1 teaspoon (5 ml) white distilled vinegar
½ teaspoon honey
¼ teaspoon salt
¼ teaspoon freshly ground black pepper
1 celery stalk, diced ⅛ inch, or 3 mm
   (½ cup, or 60 g)
2 hard-boiled large eggs, diced ¼ inch
   (6 mm)
2 scallions, chopped (¼ cup, or 25 g)

Place potatoes in a large saucepan and cover with water. Bring to a boil on high heat and continue to cook at a low boil for 6 to 8 minutes or until potatoes are fork-tender, lowering heat as necessary. Drain and spread potatoes on a plate to cool them quickly.

Blend mayonnaise, yogurt, relish, mustard, vinegar, honey, salt, and pepper in a medium bowl. Add celery, eggs, scallions, and cooled potatoes. Chill for 1 hour, up to 3 to 4 days.

 RECIPE NOTES

» This is the perfect opportunity to sneak in ½ cup (126 g) of firm tofu in place of the eggs. If your family doesn't notice the difference, you can surprise them afterward with the news that they like tofu!

» You can substitute sweet pickle relish for the dill pickle relish, as well as reducing or not using the honey. Minced pickles also work perfectly.

 TOTAL PREP AND COOK TIME: 25 MINUTES, PLUS CHILLING TIME •
YIELD: 8 SERVINGS, ½ CUP (APPROX. 106 G) EACH

PER SERVING: 133 CALORIES; 5 G TOTAL FAT; 1 G SATURATED FAT; 4 G PROTEIN; 17 G CARBOHYDRATE; 2 G DIETARY FIBER; 47 MG CHOLESTEROL.

BUSY-FAMILY DINNER SIDE SALADS

These salads make perfect complements to main dishes that don't already contain many vegetables. I encourage you to make double or triple batches of the vinaigrettes and chill in sealed jars to keep on hand for the week. Or, when you need to shave a few more minutes off mealtime prep, feel free to buy similar-tasting bottled dressings made with wholesome ingredients. I do sometimes!

SPINACH AVOCADO SALAD WITH LIME CUMIN VINAIGRETTE

FOR VINAIGRETTE:
4 teaspoons (20 ml) lime juice
½ teaspoon light agave nectar or honey
⅛ teaspoon ground cumin
⅛ teaspoon chili powder
1 pinch salt
1 pinch freshly ground black pepper
1 tablespoon (15 ml) extra-virgin olive oil

FOR SALAD:
5 cups (150 g) baby spinach
⅓ cup (50 g) halved cherry tomatoes
1 avocado, diced
3 tablespoons (35 g) roasted pepitas (shelled pumpkin seeds)

<30 TOTAL PREP AND COOK TIME: 15 MINUTES • YIELD: 4 SERVINGS, 1⅓ CUP (APPROX. 167 G) EACH

PER SERVING: 181 CALORIES; 15 G TOTAL FAT; 2 G SATURATED FAT; 6 G PROTEIN; 9 G CARBOHYDRATE; 5 G DIETARY FIBER; 0 MG CHOLESTEROL.

SPRING ARUGULA SALAD WITH PARMESAN, GRAPES & BALSAMIC BASIL VINAIGRETTE

FOR VINAIGRETTE:
1 tablespoon (15 ml) balsamic vinegar
½ teaspoon Dijon mustard
¼ teaspoon dried basil
½ teaspoon light agave nectar
1 pinch freshly ground black pepper
1 tablespoon (15 ml) extra-virgin olive oil

FOR SALAD:
5 cups (100 g) baby arugula
⅓ cup (50 g) red grapes, halved
¼ cup (45 g) jarred roasted red bell peppers, cut into strips
3 tablespoons (18 g) shaved Parmesan cheese
3 tablespoons (27 g) toasted pine nuts

<30 TOTAL PREP AND COOK TIME: 15 MINUTES • YIELD: 4 SERVINGS, 1⅓ CUP (APPROX. 167 G) EACH

PER SERVING: 109 CALORIES; 9 G TOTAL FAT; 1 G SATURATED FAT; 3 G PROTEIN; 5 G CARBOHYDRATE; 1 G DIETARY FIBER; 3 MG CHOLESTEROL.

SUMMER'S BOUNTY SALAD WITH LEMON VINAIGRETTE

FOR VINAIGRETTE:
1 tablespoon (15 ml) lemon juice
½ teaspoon Dijon mustard
½ teaspoon light agave nectar
1 pinch freshly ground black pepper
1 tablespoon (15 ml) extra-virgin olive oil

FOR SALAD:
5 cups (235 g) chopped romaine lettuce
⅓ cup (60 g) chopped tomatoes
3 tablespoons (15 g) grated Parmesan cheese
3 tablespoons (21 g) roasted almonds, chopped or sliced
3 tablespoons (30 g) minced shallots or red onion

<30 TOTAL PREP AND COOK TIME: 15 MINUTES • YIELD: 4 SERVINGS, 1⅓ CUP (APPROX. 167 G) EACH

PER SERVING: 96 CALORIES; 7 G TOTAL FAT; 1 G SATURATED FAT; 3 G PROTEIN; 5 G CARBOHYDRATE; 2 G DIETARY FIBER; 3 MG CHOLESTEROL.

FALL HARVEST SALAD WITH APPLE CIDER VINAIGRETTE

FOR VINAIGRETTE:
4 teaspoons (20 ml) apple cider vinegar
½ teaspoon Dijon mustard
½ teaspoon light agave nectar
1 pinch freshly ground black pepper
1 tablespoon (15 ml) extra-virgin olive oil

FOR SALAD:
5 cups (100 g) baby arugula
3 tablespoons (27 g) dried tart cherries or raisins
¼ cup (25 g) sliced celery
¼ cup (30 g) crumbled blue or (38 g) feta cheese
3 tablespoons (22 g) shelled pistachios, chopped
   once through

 TOTAL PREP AND COOK TIME: 15 MINUTES • YIELD: 4 SERVINGS, 1⅓ CUP (APPROX. 167 G) EACH

PER SERVING: 123 CALORIES; 8 G TOTAL FAT; 2 G SATURATED FAT; 3 G PROTEIN; 10 G CARBOHYDRATE; 1 G DIETARY FIBER; 8 MG CHOLESTEROL.

KALE & CARROT SLAW WITH GINGER VINAIGRETTE

FOR VINAIGRETTE:
3 tablespoons (45 ml) rice vinegar
2 teaspoons (5 g) grated ginger
2 teaspoons (10 ml) reduced sodium soy sauce
2 teaspoons (13 g) light agave nectar
1½ teaspoons (6 g) Chinese mustard
⅛ teaspoon freshly ground black pepper
2 tablespoons (28 ml) extra-virgin olive oil

FOR SALAD:
7 cups (470 g) shredded kale
½ cup (55 g) shredded carrots
2 scallions, cut crosswise into 1-inch (2.5 cm) sections,
   thinly sliced lengthwise
1 tablespoon (8 g) toasted sesame seeds

TOTAL PREP AND COOK TIME: 15 MINUTES • YIELD: 4 SERVINGS, 1⅓ CUP (APPROX. 167 G) EACH

PER SERVING: 149 CALORIES; 8 G TOTAL FAT; 1 G SATURATED FAT; 14 G PROTEIN; 17 G CARBOHYDRATE; 13 G DIETARY FIBER; 0 MG CHOLESTEROL.

TO MAKE VINAIGRETTES: Blend all vinaigrette ingredients, except oil, in a bowl. Slowly drizzle in the oil while whisking to blend in completely. You can also shake all ingredients together in a sealed jar for a no-clean-up option.

TO MAKE SALADS: Place salad ingredients in a medium bowl, pour in vinaigrette, and toss together. Serve immediately if making any one of the first four salads. For kale salad, allow to rest 15 minutes before serving to tenderize.

RECIPE NOTES

Toast pine nuts in batches and store them in the fridge for future use to save time. To toast, place the pine nuts in a large frying pan over medium-low heat. Stir every 30 seconds until toasted all around. Stay close to the stove, as the scent will remind you to stir often and prevent a burned batch.

CHOPPED SALAD WITH ISRAELI COUSCOUS, SMOKED SALMON & CREAMY PESTO

The best salad I ever ate was at Citizen Public House, a trendy restaurant in Scottsdale, Arizona. I tailored that recipe for the home cook by shrinking prep time and using more available ingredients. This salad works well as an entrée paired with soup or crusty bread, as a party dish to pass around, or divided into smaller servings, as a starter course at a dinner party.

FOR SALAD:

1⅓ cups (209 g) cooked Israeli (pearled) couscous (whole-grain preferred)

3 teaspoons (15 ml) expeller-pressed grapeseed or canola oil, divided

1 ear of corn (or 1 cup [164 g] frozen corn, thawed only, not blistered)

4 cups (80 g) arugula, chopped (or [120 g] baby spinach)

1 cup (180 g) diced tomatoes (about 1 large)

1 (4-ounce, or 115 g) package smoked wild Alaskan salmon, diced ¼ inch, or 6 mm (about 1 cup)

½ cup (75 g) golden raisins, chopped through twice

¼ cup (20 g) shredded Asiago cheese (or Parmesan)

¼ cup (35 g) roasted pepitas (shelled pumpkin seeds, or use chopped roasted almonds [25g])

FOR DRESSING:

3 tablespoons (45 ml) low-fat milk

2 tablespoons (28 g) olive oil mayonnaise

2 tablespoons (30 g) nonfat plain Greek yogurt

1 tablespoon + 1 teaspoon (20 g) basil pesto

1 tablespoon (10 g) minced shallots

1 teaspoon (5 ml) lemon juice

¼ teaspoon freshly ground black pepper

TO MAKE THE SALAD: Prepare couscous according to directions on package. Toss with 2 teaspoons (10 ml) of the oil to prevent sticking and spread mixture on a plate to cool it quickly. Heat a medium sauté pan over medium heat and add 1 teaspoon (5 ml) of oil. Place the ear of corn into the pan and blister on one side, about 1 minute. Continue to cook and turn corn until all sides are blistered; remove pan from heat and let cool slightly. Stand the cob up on a cutting board and holding it firmly, cut the kernels off the cob.

TO MAKE THE DRESSING: Whisk together all of the dressing ingredients.

When ready to serve, combine the couscous, corn, and remaining salad ingredients and pour the dressing on top. Toss well. Salad may be served immediately and will stay fresh for a few hours.

 GO GREEN

Corn and tomatoes peak in summer and fall. Substitute 1 cup (164 g) frozen, canned, or freeze-dried corn (no need to blister) and ¼ cup (45 g) sun-dried tomatoes in oil, drained, during the off season.

 RECIPE NOTE

For an impressive table presentation, spoon lines of each ingredient in a 9 x 13-inch (23 x 33 cm) glass pan or large platter. Cover and refrigerate until ready to serve.

TOTAL PREP AND COOK TIME: 45 MINUTES • YIELD: 4 MAIN DISH (2 CUPS, OR APPROX. 284 G) OR 8 SIDE DISH (1 CUP, OR APPROX. 142 G) SERVINGS

PER SERVING: 379 CALORIES; 18 G TOTAL FAT; 3 G SATURATED FAT; 18 G PROTEIN; 41 G CARBOHYDRATE; 4 G DIETARY FIBER; 20 MG CHOLESTEROL.

"MIX IT ONCE, MILK IT FOR THE WEEK" GARDEN CAESAR PASTA SALAD

I grew up eating packaged pasta mixes, and as an adult, I found myself still craving them from time to time. I discovered that Scarlet loves them, too, so I decided it was time to give this recipe a makeover with more nutritious ingredients. One of my favorite pasta brands is made largely of legume flour, which adds protein, making this salad a meal in itself.

FOR PASTA:

1 medium red bell pepper, sliced ¼-inch (6 mm)-thick (about 1 cup, or 150 g)

½ medium carrot, cut into two 2-inch (5 cm) pieces

5 cups (700 g) cooked (3 cups [315 g] dry) whole-grain farfalle (bow-tie) pasta, tossed in extra-virgin olive oil to prevent sticking, cooled

⅓ cup (33 g) grated Parmesan cheese

1 tablespoon (4 g) chopped Italian flat-leaf parsley (or 1 teaspoon [0.3 g] dried parsley)

1 cup (30 g) Caesar croutons, chopped if large (whole-grain preferred)

FOR DRESSING:

¼ cup (60 g) olive oil mayonnaise (or light mayonnaise)

1 tablespoon (15 g) Dijon mustard

3 anchovies (optional)

3 tablespoons (45 ml) lemon juice (or less if you prefer a milder dressing)

1 tablespoon (15 ml) red wine vinegar

½ teaspoon garlic powder

½ teaspoon freshly ground black pepper

½ teaspoon salt

¼ teaspoon Worcestershire sauce

1 tablespoon (15 ml) extra-virgin olive oil

TO MAKE THE SALAD: Place bell pepper slices in a food processor and pulse 15 times or until finely chopped, scraping down the sides halfway through. Spoon chopped peppers into a large mixing bowl. Repeat with carrot. Place pasta, cheese, and parsley in the bowl.

TO MAKE THE DRESSING: Combine mayonnaise, mustard, anchovies, lemon juice, vinegar, garlic powder, pepper, salt, and Worcestershire sauce in the food processor, whirring until smooth while drizzling in the oil. Add dressing to salad and stir until well blended. Chill for 1 hour, up to 4 days. Garnish with croutons right before serving.

 RECIPE NOTE

Finely mincing ingredients with a knife can substitute for using a food processor. An immersion blender may be used to blend the dressing; or the anchovies and garlic can be finely minced by hand.

 GO GREEN

Bell peppers are available year-round in warm climates, peaking in spring and summer in colder regions. Substitute ½ cup (90 g) of jarred, chopped, roasted bell peppers in fall and winter.

TOTAL PREP AND COOK TIME: 40 MINUTES • YIELD: 8 SERVINGS, ¾ CUP (APPROX. 210 G) EACH

PER SERVING: 213 CALORIES; 7 G TOTAL FAT; 1 G SATURATED FAT; 8 G PROTEIN; 30 G CARBOHYDRATE; 3 G DIETARY FIBER; 7 MG CHOLESTEROL.

LENTIL SALAD WITH BELL PEPPER, AVOCADO & APPLE CIDER VINAIGRETTE

Cooking dried lentils takes less time than you might think, and in this recipe, I presoaked the lentils to reduce the cooking time by half. Lentils are an economical and abundant source of protein, serving as a nutritious main or side dish.

1 cup (192 g) dry brown (or green) lentils
1 bay leaf
1 cup (150 g) diced red bell pepper
¾ cup (90 g) diced celery
1 avocado, diced
¼ cup (40 g) diced red onion
¼ cup (4 g) chopped cilantro
3 tablespoons (45 ml) apple cider vinegar
1 tablespoon (15 ml) extra-virgin olive oil
2 teaspoons (6 g) jalapeño, membranes
   and seed removed, minced
1 teaspoon (5 ml) lime juice
1 teaspoon (3 g) ground cumin
½ teaspoon salt
¼ teaspoon freshly ground black pepper

Cover lentils with at least 1 inch (2.5 cm) of water and soak for 2 to 3 hours so that they swell and double in size. Drain and rinse. Place lentils in a medium saucepan, cover with 1 inch (2.5 cm) of water, add bay leaf, and bring to a boil on high heat. Cook for 8 minutes (longer for older, drier lentils) until tender, reducing heat as necessary. Rinse lentils with cold water, drain well, and place in a large bowl. Add remaining ingredients and stir. Chill for at least 30 minutes, up to 3 days.

 GO CLEAN

Several studies have demonstrated that vinegar may help lower glucose levels, which can be beneficial to people managing diabetes. Regardless of the research, apple cider vinegar lends a tart yet sweet and calorie-free addition to balance recipes.

+ RECIPE NOTE

Here's the no-fuss, no-mess way to cut an avocado: Cut through the flesh lengthwise and around the pit with a knife and twist apart the 2 halves. If dicing, score the flesh by cutting small squares without piercing through the skin. Scoop the avocado out completely with a spoon, making sure to scrape up the darkest green part closest to the skin, which contains the highest concentration of nutrients such as beta-carotene.

 TOTAL PREP AND COOK TIME: 25 MINUTES, PLUS SOAKING TIME • YIELD: 9 SERVINGS, ½ CUP (APPROX. 99 G) EACH

PER SERVING: 134 CALORIES; 5 G TOTAL FAT; 1 G SATURATED FAT; 6 G PROTEIN; 17 G CARBOHYDRATE; 9 G DIETARY FIBER; 0 MG CHOLESTEROL.

CUCUMBER QUINOA SALAD WITH FETA CHEESE, OLIVES, MINT & OREGANO

Quinoa is an ancient Incan grain and a complete source of vegan protein, providing all of your daily essential amino acids. Just 1 cup (185 g) of cooked quinoa offers 8 grams of protein, 5 grams of fiber, 15 percent of your Daily Value for iron, and 6 percent of your Daily Value for potassium, a nutrient for which many people don't reach the recommended requirement. This salad serves as a refreshing, light, yet satisfying main or side dish. Find quinoa in the natural food section of your grocery store, near the grains.

1 cup (173 g) dry quinoa, debris and
    discolored seeds removed
1½ cups (355 ml) organic or reduced
    sodium vegetable broth
1 large cucumber, peeled, seeded, and
    chopped (1½ cups, or 205 g)
1 large tomato, seeded and chopped
    (1 cup, or 180 g)
⅓ cup (50 g) crumbled feta cheese
¼ cup (25 g) pitted kalamata olives, sliced
2 tablespoons (28 ml) red wine vinegar
2 tablespoons (28 ml) extra-virgin olive oil
1 tablespoon (6 g) chopped mint (or
    1 teaspoon [0.5 g] dried mint)
½ teaspoon salt
¼ teaspoon dried oregano

Place quinoa in a medium saucepan, cover with water, and let soak for 5 minutes to prevent stickiness. Stir, then rinse in a colander with cool water, and drain. Return quinoa to the saucepan and add broth. Bring to a boil on high heat; reduce heat to low, cover, and cook for 20 minutes until quinoa is tender and liquid is completely absorbed. Spread quinoa on a plate to cool it quickly.

Place quinoa in a medium bowl and mix with the remaining ingredients. Chill for at least 30 minutes, up to 3 days.

 GO GREEN

When domestic cucumbers and tomatoes are out of season in your area, try substituting 1½ cups (360 g) chickpeas, ¼ cup (40 g) minced red onion, and ¼ cup (45 g) sun-dried tomatoes in olive oil, drained and chopped.

TOTAL PREP AND COOK TIME: 1 HOUR • YIELD: 11 SERVINGS, ½ CUP (APPROX. 60 G) EACH

PER SERVING: 126 CALORIES; 5 G TOTAL FAT; 1 G SATURATED FAT; 4 G PROTEIN; 16 G CARBOHYDRATE; 2 G DIETARY FIBER; 4 MG CHOLESTEROL.

ARUGULA & SHRIMP SALAD WITH ORANGE VINAIGRETTE

Enjoy this satisfying salad in the spring and imagine the pounds melting off in time for summer fun.

FOR VINAIGRETTE:

3 tablespoons (45 ml) freshly squeezed
    orange juice (juice of 1 orange)
2 teaspoons (10 ml) rice vinegar
1 teaspoon (6 g) honey
½ teaspoon Dijon mustard
1 tablespoon (15 ml) extra-virgin olive oil
1 pinch salt

FOR SALAD:

5 ounces (140 g) cooked shrimp (about
    1¼ cups), peeled, tails removed
4 cups (80 g) lightly packed fresh arugula
    (or [120 g] baby spinach)
8 thin slices Asiago or Parmesan cheese,
    halved diagonally
¼ cup (33 g) slivered dried apricots
1 medium shallot, thinly sliced
2 tablespoons (14 g) sliced almonds,
    toasted
¼ teaspoon freshly ground black pepper

TO MAKE THE VINAIGRETTE: Whisk orange juice, vinegar, honey, and mustard in a medium bowl. Drizzle in the oil while whisking. Add warm shrimp and marinate for a few minutes in the dressing.

TO MAKE THE SALAD: Combine arugula, cheese, apricots, shallot, almonds, and pepper in another medium bowl. Pour in vinaigrette, holding back the shrimp. Toss salad with tongs and divide among salad bowls. Place shrimp atop salad in each bowl and enjoy immediately.

GO GREEN

Domestic navel oranges peak from November to the end of May, and Valencia oranges peak from April through early fall.

RECIPE NOTE

You can use frozen, precooked tiny salad shrimp or medium shrimp, thawed. Or, to cook your own, bring a medium pot of water to a boil. Add a pinch of salt to the water and then add the shrimp; turn off the heat immediately and remove the shrimp as soon as they are opaque in the center, after about 5 minutes for medium shrimp.

 TOTAL PREP AND COOK TIME: 25 MINUTES • YIELD: 2 MAIN DISH SERVINGS OR 4 APPETIZERS

PER SERVING: 330 CALORIES; 17 G TOTAL FAT; 5 G SATURATED FAT; 22 G PROTEIN; 23 G CARBOHYDRATE; 3 G DIETARY FIBER; 154 MG CHOLESTEROL.

GREEN BEAN, ARTICHOKE & WHITE BEAN SALAD WITH RED WINE VINAIGRETTE

My assistant Kim's ten-year-old son loved this salad and asked, "When is Bring Your Son to Work Day?" Enjoy this salad as a side dish with seafood or a light sandwich or increase the portion size to serve as a lunchtime meal in itself.

1 cup (100 g) green beans, trimmed, cut into 1-inch (2.5 cm) pieces

1 (8-ounce, or 225 g) package frozen artichoke heart quarters (about 1¼ cups)

1 (15-ounce, or 425 g) can white beans (cannellini, navy, or great northern), rinsed and drained

1 large tomato, diced medium (about 1 cup, or 180 g)

¼ cup (15 g) chopped parsley

2 scallions, sliced

2 tablespoons (28 ml) red wine vinegar

2 tablespoons (28 ml) extra-virgin olive oil

1½ teaspoons (7 g) Dijon mustard

½ teaspoon salt

½ teaspoon dried basil

¼ teaspoon freshly ground black pepper

¼ teaspoon garlic powder

¼ teaspoon dried oregano

Fill a medium saucepan halfway with water and bring to a boil over high heat. Add a pinch of salt and the green beans and boil for 4 minutes. Add artichokes and continue to boil for 5 minutes until vegetables are tender. Drain and add vegetables to a bowl of ice water to cool quickly. Drain again. Add vegetables and remaining ingredients to a medium mixing bowl and mix well. Chill for at least 2 hours, up to 4 days.

 GO GREEN

Green beans peak during summer months and are available longer in frost-free regions. When domestic varieties aren't available, substitute with frozen cut green beans and cook according to package directions. Reduced sodium or salt-free canned beans work well, too.

 RECIPE NOTE

You can substitute canned or jarred artichokes for frozen, which eliminates the need to boil.

 **TOTAL PREP AND COOK TIME: 30 MINUTES, PLUS CHILLING TIME •
YIELD: 9 SERVINGS, ½ CUP (APPROX. 111 G) EACH**

PER SERVING: 81 CALORIES; 3 G TOTAL FAT; TRACE SATURATED FAT; 4 G PROTEIN; 11 G CARBOHYDRATE; 4 G DIETARY FIBER; 0 MG CHOLESTEROL.

WHOLE-WHEAT COUSCOUS TABBOULEH WITH TOASTED ALMONDS

From tabbouleh to kibbe to lebon khar, home-cooked meals always tasted amazing at my Lebanese grandma's and great-grandma's homes. My busy-family twist on the classic uses quick-cooking whole-wheat couscous instead of long-soaking wheat bulgur. Available in small boxes or bulk bins, couscous is a low-commitment purchase, another reason I think you'll want to make this recipe again and again.

2 cups (475 ml) organic or reduced sodium vegetable broth

1 cup (175 g) dry whole-wheat Israeli (pearled) couscous

2 medium tomatoes, chopped (1 cup, or 180 g)

1½ cups (90 g) Italian flat-leaf parsley, roughly chopped

¼ cup (40 g) red onion, chopped small

2 tablespoons (12 g) roughly chopped mint

2 tablespoons (28 ml) lemon juice

2 tablespoons (28 ml) extra-virgin olive oil

½ teaspoon freshly ground black pepper

¼ teaspoon salt

¼ cup (28 g) sliced or slivered almonds, toasted

Bring broth to a boil in a medium saucepan over high heat. Stir in couscous, reduce heat to low, and simmer for 8 minutes. Remove couscous from heat and fluff with a fork. Pour couscous onto a large plate in an even layer and draw lines through it with a spoon to cool it quickly. Add tomatoes, parsley, onion, mint, lemon juice, oil, pepper, and salt. Chill for at least 1 hour until ready to serve, up to 3 days. Right before serving, sprinkle with almonds.

 RECIPE NOTES

» Stir in 1 (14-ounce, or 390 g) can of chickpeas and serve over a small bed of chopped romaine lettuce for a substantial main dish. Adjust seasonings as needed.

» You can find whole-wheat Israeli couscous in the kosher or rice section of the grocery store (even though it's essentially wheat pasta). You can substitute regular Israeli couscous or small-grain whole-wheat couscous. Adjust the cooking procedure as indicated on the package.

TOTAL PREP AND COOK TIME: 35 MINUTES • YIELD: 8 SERVINGS, ½ CUP (APPROX. 128 G) EACH

PER SERVING: 150 CALORIES; 6 G TOTAL FAT; 1 G SATURATED FAT; 4 G PROTEIN; 23 G CARBOHYDRATE; 2 G DIETARY FIBER; 0 MG CHOLESTEROL.

WHOLE-WHEAT ORZO SALAD WITH SPINACH, GRAPES & PARMESAN

The beautiful balance of sweet, sour, and salty tastes comes through in this simple salad. You might want to make a double batch and enjoy leftovers the next day, since hearty spinach stands up to the light lemon vinaigrette.

1 cup (220 g) dry whole-wheat orzo

2 tablespoons (28 ml) extra-virgin olive oil, divided

2 cups (60 g) roughly chopped baby spinach

1¼ cups (188 g) halved seedless red grapes

½ cup (60 g) diced celery

¼ cup (30 g) shelled pistachios, chopped once through

¼ cup (25 g) thinly sliced scallions

¼ cup (20 g) shaved or thinly sliced Parmesan cheese

2 tablespoons (28 ml) lemon juice

¼ teaspoon salt

¼ teaspoon freshly ground black pepper

Fill a medium saucepan halfway with water and bring to a boil on high heat. Stir in orzo, add 1 pinch of salt, and boil for 8 to 10 minutes until al dente. Drain in a fine colander and pour onto a large plate. Drizzle on 1 tablespoon (15 ml) of oil, separating orzo into sections with a spoon to speed cooling to room temperature.

Toss together in a medium bowl the cooled orzo, remaining tablespoon (15 ml) of oil, spinach, grapes, celery, pistachios, scallions, Parmesan cheese, lemon juice, salt, and pepper. Eat immediately or chill until ready to serve, up to 2 days.

 GO GREEN

Domestically grown table grape season begins in late spring and ends in December. During the off season substitute ½ cup (75 g) of raisins or 1 cup (75 g) of red-skinned diced pears or apples that have been dipped in water with a little added lemon juice to prevent browning.

 RECIPE NOTES

» Find orzo in the kosher or rice (even though it's wheat pasta) section of the grocery store. You can substitute regular orzo or barley cooked according to the package directions if whole-wheat orzo is unavailable.

» If you are using a colander with large holes, line the bottom with a coffee filter or cheesecloth to prevent the orzo from falling through.

 TOTAL PREP AND COOK TIME: 30 MINUTES • YIELD: 4 SERVINGS, 1 CUP (APPROX. 223 G) EACH

PER SERVING: 345 CALORIES; 12 G TOTAL FAT; 2 G SATURATED FAT; 12 G PROTEIN; 51 G CARBOHYDRATE; 6 G DIETARY FIBER; 4 MG CHOLESTEROL.

CROWD-PLEASING FRESH SPINACH, RED BELL PEPPER & ARTICHOKE DIP

Even my Wisconsin "cheese-head" Uncle Jeff asked me for this recipe after he tasted it, so you know it's got to be good! One of my best friends, Kimberly, called this dish "dreamy" and enjoyed using fresh spinach instead of squeezing the frozen stuff.

2 teaspoons (10 ml) extra-virgin olive oil

1 cup (160 g) finely chopped onion

1 diced red bell pepper (about 1 cup, or 150 g)

1 teaspoon (3 g) minced garlic

12 cups (360 g) fresh baby spinach, chopped

1 (8-ounce, or 225 g) package light cream cheese

½ cup (115 g) light mayonnaise

¾ cup (75 g) + 2 tablespoons (10 g) grated Parmesan cheese, divided

1 (14-ounce, or 390 g) can artichoke hearts, drained, roughly chopped

½ cup (57 g) shredded Monterey Jack cheese

¼ cup (15 g) chopped Italian flat-leaf parsley

1 tablespoon (15 ml) lemon juice

1 teaspoon (5 ml) hot sauce

¼ teaspoon salt

¼ teaspoon freshly ground black pepper

1 scallion, thinly sliced (2 tablespoons, or 12 g)

Whole-grain crackers or tortilla chips, vegetable sticks

Preheat oven to 350°F (180°C, or gas mark 4). Heat a large pot over medium heat and add oil. Add onion, red pepper, and garlic, and cook until transparent, about 7 minutes. Stir in spinach and cook for 5 minutes. Remove from heat and stir in cream cheese until melted. Add mayonnaise, ¾ cup (75 g) of Parmesan cheese, artichokes, Monterey Jack cheese, parsley, lemon juice, hot sauce, salt, and pepper. Transfer to a 1½-quart (1.4 L) casserole dish and sprinkle with remaining 2 tablespoons (10 g) of Parmesan cheese. Bake until bubbly around the edges and golden on top, about 35 minutes. Sprinkle with scallions and serve warm with dippers.

 RECIPE NOTE

Save chopping time by pulsing vegetables separately in a food processor.

TOTAL PREP AND COOK TIME: 65 MINUTES • YIELD: 20 SERVINGS, ¼ CUP (APPROX. 78 G) EACH

PER SERVING: 91 CALORIES; 6 G TOTAL FAT; 3 G SATURATED FAT; 4 G PROTEIN; 5 G CARBOHYDRATE; 2 G DIETARY FIBER; 14 MG CHOLESTEROL.

 GO CLEAN

Be sure your spinach comes from domestic sources. If not, stir in 2 (10-ounce, or 280 g) boxes of frozen chopped spinach, thawed, squeezing out all of the water.

CREAMY AVOCADO, TOMATO & BLACK BEAN DIP

If you love traditional queso bean dip, I think you will really appreciate that this recipe delivers creaminess and full flavor, but with a lot less saturated fat and more fruits, vegetables, and nutrients. Serve it as a dip, slather it on whole-grain nachos, or use it as a filling for burritos.

1 teaspoon (5 ml) extra-virgin olive oil

½ small onion, finely chopped (about ½ cup, or 80 g)

1 teaspoon (3 g) minced garlic

1 large tomato, chopped small (about 1 cup, 180 g)

1 (15-ounce, or 425 g) can black beans, rinsed and drained

¼ cup (65 g) salsa

1 tablespoon + 1½ teaspoons (22.5 ml) lime juice

¼ cup (4 g) chopped cilantro

1½ teaspoons (7.5 ml) hot sauce

½ teaspoon ground cumin

¼ teaspoon ancho chili powder (or regular chili powder)

¼ teaspoon liquid amino acids or reduced sodium soy sauce

¼ teaspoon freshly ground black pepper

½ avocado, diced

¼ cup (60 ml) organic or reduced sodium vegetable broth

Whole-grain tortilla chips, sweet bell pepper strips

Heat a large skillet over medium-low heat and add oil. When oil is shimmering, add onion and garlic and cook until translucent, about 5 minutes. Add tomato and cook for 2 minutes. Stir in beans, salsa, lime juice, cilantro, hot sauce, cumin, chili powder, amino acids, and pepper and heat through. Remove pan from heat and place half of the contents in a blender with avocado and broth; purée until smooth. Add puréed mixture back to the pan to reheat, stirring occasionally. Serve warm with chips and peppers.

 GO CLEAN

All tortilla chips are not created equal. Look for "whole corn" listed as the first ingredient, instead of corn flour. Whole corn includes the germ and bran and contains more naturally occurring nutrients than refined corn flour. Since sodium contents can vary, choose chips with fewer than 140 milligrams. Finally, opt for chips made with expeller-pressed (mechanically extracted) oils instead of those extracted with hexane, an industrial chemical classified as a hazardous air pollutant.

 TOTAL PREP AND COOK TIME: 30 MINUTES • YIELD: 8 SERVINGS, ¼ CUP (APPROX. 104 G) EACH

PER SERVING: 137 CALORIES; 4 G TOTAL FAT; 1 G SATURATED FAT; 4 G PROTEIN; 11 G CARBOHYDRATE; 4 G DIETARY FIBER; 0 MG CHOLESTEROL.

7-LAYER LEMON HUMMUS & PESTO YOGURT DIP

Mexican 7-layer dip is one of my all-time snack favorites, and my Mediterranean spin offers a delightful alternative. The hummus recipe within the recipe may stand alone as your go-to dip for vegetable crudités. My sister-in-law Maria serves hummus at social gatherings and prefers this crowd-pleasing rendition because it's refreshing and adds a serving of vegetables. If you find yourself in a time crunch, use store-bought hummus. Your secret will be safe with me.

1 (15-ounce, or 425 g) can chickpeas, rinsed and drained

3 tablespoons (45 g) tahini (sesame seed paste found in the ethnic food section, or use unsweetened almond butter)

1 lemon separated into 1 teaspoon (2 g) grated zest, 3 tablespoons (45 ml) juice

3 tablespoons (45 ml) organic or reduced sodium vegetable broth

½ teaspoon salt

¼ teaspoon garlic powder

¼ teaspoon freshly ground black pepper

1 tablespoon (15 ml) extra-virgin olive oil

1 cup (230 g) nonfat plain Greek yogurt

⅓ cup (87 g) basil pesto

1 cup (80 g) shredded (not grated) Parmesan cheese (or use crumbled feta for a stronger taste)

1 large tomato, seeded, diced ¼ inch, or 6 mm (1 cup, or 180 g)

1 small cucumber, peeled, seeded with a spoon, and diced (about ¾ cup, or 101 g)

⅓ cup (33 g) thinly sliced scallions

⅓ cup (33 g) pitted kalamata olives, sliced

Grilled or toasted whole-grain pita chips or flatbread torn into pieces, romaine hearts

TO MAKE THE HUMMUS: Purée chickpeas, tahini, lemon juice, lemon zest, broth, salt, garlic powder, and pepper in a food processor until smooth. Drizzle in olive oil. Spread hummus evenly in the bottom of a 9 x 9-inch (23 x 23 cm) glass dish.

Stir together yogurt and pesto and spoon over hummus. Evenly sprinkle the cheese, followed by single layers of tomatoes, cucumbers, scallions, and olives. Enjoy this dish on the same or the next day for optimal freshness.

 RECIPE NOTE

For a more festive look, use a trifle-style glass bowl rather than a square baking dish. It makes for a great-looking potluck contribution.

 GO CLEAN

Read the ingredient list closely on bottled pesto, looking for those made with olive oil instead of soybean oil for a heart-healthier fat.

 <30 TOTAL PREP AND COOK TIME: 30 MINUTES • YIELD: 20 SERVINGS, ¼ CUP (APPROX. 61 G) EACH

PER SERVING: 77 CALORIES; 5 G TOTAL FAT; 1 G SATURATED FAT; 4 G PROTEIN; 5 G CARBOHYDRATE; 1 G DIETARY FIBER; 4 MG CHOLESTEROL.

LIME CUMIN DEVILED EGGS

Did you know that eggs are the most absorbable form of protein compared to all other foods? These satisfying deviled eggs may serve as a main dish or heavy appetizer for an easygoing brunch, play date, or cocktail party. Just ask my friend Lisa who maintains a kosher kitchen and begs me to bring these to all of her parties.

1 dozen large eggs
½ cup (115 g) light mayonnaise
¼ cup (45 g) jarred roasted red bell peppers
2 teaspoons (10 ml) lime juice
1 teaspoon (5 g) Dijon mustard
¼ teaspoon ground cumin
¼ teaspoon salt
¼ teaspoon freshly ground black pepper
⅛ teaspoon chili powder (more for spicier eggs)
24 1-inch (2.5 cm) roasted red bell pepper strips
2 tablespoons (6 g) chives, thinly sliced

Place eggs in a pot and cover with water. Bring to a low boil over high heat. Reduce heat as needed to maintain a low boil for 12 minutes. Remove eggs from heat and carefully drain pot. Fill pot with cold water and a handful of ice to cool the eggs quickly. Peel the eggs and slice them in half lengthwise. Gently remove yolks and place them in a medium bowl. Arrange egg whites on a sheet pan lined with a paper towel.

Blend yolks, mayonnaise, ¼ cup (45 g) of jarred peppers, lime juice, mustard, cumin, salt, pepper, and chili powder in a food processor (or with a whisk or potato masher) until smooth. Spoon filling into a small resealable plastic bag and cut ¼ inch (6 mm) from either bottom corner. Twist bag to push all of the filling into one corner and squeeze to fill egg whites with yolk mixture.

Place bell pepper strips diagonally across each egg and sprinkle with chives. Cover lightly and chill until ready to serve, up to 4 days.

TOTAL PREP AND COOK TIME: 1 HOUR • YIELD: 24 SERVINGS, ½ EGG EACH

PER SERVING: 52 CALORIES; 4 G TOTAL FAT; 1 G SATURATED FAT; 3 G PROTEIN; TRACE CARBOHYDRATE; TRACE DIETARY FIBER; 93 MG CHOLESTEROL.

TOMATO-STUDDED GUACAMOLE WITH SCALLIONS & CHILI

I perfected this dip during a stint as a private chef in my boss's open-air kitchen overlooking the beaches of San Jose del Cabo, Mexico. To select a perfectly ripe avocado, give it a gentle squeeze in the palm of your hand—it should be firm, yet yield slightly to pressure.

3 ripe large avocados

1 scallion, green part only, thinly sliced (about 2 tablespoons, or 13 g)

2 tablespoons (2 g) chopped cilantro or Italian flat-leaf parsley

1 tablespoon (15 ml) lime juice

2 teaspoons (6 g) minced jalapeño with seeds and inner membranes removed

¼ teaspoon chili powder

¼ teaspoon salt

¼ teaspoon freshly ground black pepper

⅛ teaspoon garlic powder (or ½ teaspoon fresh garlic for a stronger taste)

1 tiny pinch oregano, crumbled between fingers (optional)

1 large tomato, seeded and diced ¼ inch, or 6 mm (about 1 cup, or 180 g)

Whole-grain tortilla chips

Cut avocados in half lengthwise going around the pit, twist to separate the halves, and then remove the seed. With a tablespoon, scoop the flesh into a medium bowl. Mash avocado flesh with a whisk or potato masher until chunky. Stir in scallions, cilantro, lime juice, jalapeño, chili powder, salt, pepper, garlic powder, and oregano. Taste-test with a tortilla chip and adjust seasonings as desired.

Cover with plastic wrap pressed directly on the surface of the guacamole to prevent browning until ready to serve. Upon serving, stir in half of the tomatoes* and sprinkle the other half on top. Serve with chips.

RECIPE NOTE

*Since tomatoes release water when in contact with salt, only stir in enough tomatoes for the amount of guacamole you will enjoy immediately to prevent a watered-down version.

GO GREEN

» Avocados are in season spring, summer, and early fall.

» When tomato quality diminishes in the colder months, try stirring in pomegranate seeds instead. To seed a pomegranate, cut off the top part of the stem end. With a knife, score the skin's surface into quarters from top to bottom. Pull the quarters apart with your hands. Bend back the skin and scoop out the seeds over a bowl or holding the pomegranate skin side up, whack the skin with a spoon so that the seeds fall out.

 TOTAL PREP AND COOK TIME: 15 MINUTES • YIELD: 8 SERVINGS, ¼ CUP (APPROX. 25 G) EACH

PER SERVING: 127 CALORIES; 11 G TOTAL FAT; 2 G SATURATED FAT; 2 G PROTEIN; 8 G CARBOHYDRATE; 5 G DIETARY FIBER; 0 MG CHOLESTEROL.

SCARLET-APPROVED LEMON CILANTRO EDAMAME HUMMUS

I knew I hit a home run when I tested this recipe on Scarlet and heard her say, "I want more." Substituting young green soybeans for chickpeas offers a refreshing variation from the usual. And did you know that soybeans offer a complete vegan protein? Instead of serving this as a dip, fill whole-wheat wraps with hummus, baby spinach, tomatoes, and cucumber.

1½ cups (225 g) frozen shelled edamame
1 clove garlic (or 1 teaspoon [3 g] minced)
1 teaspoon (3 g) jalapeño with membrane removed, seeded, cut into chunks
½ cup (8 g) cilantro sprigs
3 tablespoons (45 g) tahini (roasted sesame seed butter, or use unsweetened almond butter)
3 tablespoons + 2 teaspoons (55 ml) freshly squeezed lemon juice (or use less to taste)
1 teaspoon (2 g) grated lemon zest
½ teaspoon ground cumin
¼ teaspoon ground coriander
¼ + ⅛ teaspoon salt
⅛ teaspoon freshly ground black pepper
1 tablespoon (15 ml) extra-virgin olive oil
Whole-grain tortilla or pita chips, vegetable crudités

Fill a medium saucepan halfway with water and bring to a boil. Add edamame, bring back to a boil, and cook for 7 minutes until tender. Reserve cooking water. Fill a small bowl with ice water. Mince garlic and jalapeño in a food processor. Remove cooked edamame immediately with a slotted spoon and transfer to ice water to cool and to retain bright color. Drain ice water and add edamame to the food processor, along with cilantro, tahini, lemon juice, lemon zest, cumin, coriander, salt, and pepper. Run for 30 seconds. Scrape down the sides of the bowl and add up to 3 tablespoons (45 ml) of cooking liquid to adjust consistency. Run the food processor for another 30 seconds while drizzling the oil into the mixture. Chill until ready to serve, up to 4 days. Enjoy with chips and vegetables.

 TOTAL PREP AND COOK TIME: 30 MINUTES • YIELD: 10 SERVINGS, 2 TABLESPOONS (30 G) EACH

PER SERVING: 72 CALORIES; 5 G TOTAL FAT; TRACE SATURATED FAT; 3 G PROTEIN; 4 G CARBOHYDRATE; 2 G DIETARY FIBER; 0 MG CHOLESTEROL.

 RECIPE NOTE

Find tahini in the natural food section with nut butters. Be sure to stir it very well before use.

PINTO BEAN & AVOCADO TAQUITOS

I can't seem to get enough of chips, salsa, guacamole, and Mexican restaurants in general, so I created this recipe to fulfill my cravings at home without the added calories from deep-frying. I knew this taquito dish was a winner when I found myself grabbing them right out of the fridge for lunches on the go. The creaminess of the beans and avocado satisfies the craving for cheese.

1 (15-ounce, or 425 g) can pinto beans, rinsed and drained

1 avocado, scooped from skin, pit removed

3 tablespoons (30 g) minced red onion

2 tablespoons (14 g) diced sun-dried tomatoes

1 tablespoon (15 ml) lemon juice

2 teaspoons (10 ml) reduced sodium soy sauce

¼ teaspoon ground cumin

¼ teaspoon freshly ground pepper

⅛ teaspoon salt

12 corn tortillas

2 tablespoons + 1½ teaspoons (35 ml) expeller-pressed grapeseed or canola oil

Taco sauce or salsa, for dipping

Preheat oven to 425°F (220°C, or gas mark 7) and line a large sheet pan with parchment paper or cooking oil spray. In a medium bowl, smash beans a few times with a potato masher. Add avocado and mash a few more times, leaving bite-size pieces. Stir in onion, tomatoes, lemon juice, soy sauce, cumin, pepper, and salt.

Warm half of the tortillas in 2 stacks of 3 each in the microwave until soft, about 30 seconds. Pour oil into a small bowl and brush both sides of each tortilla. Determine which side of each tortilla is curving inward and make that the inside. Spoon 2 tablespoons (28 g) of filling in a line near the center of each tortilla, leaving ½ inch (1.3 cm) from each end. Roll tortillas tightly and place them seam side down on the pan. Warm remaining half of tortillas when needed. Bake 21 minutes until golden. Serve hot with taco sauce or salsa.

 RECIPE NOTE

To prep this recipe ahead of time, you can mix the filling and lay plastic wrap directly on the surface to prevent the avocados from browning. Brush and fill the tortillas right before baking.

TOTAL PREP AND COOK TIME: 40 MINUTES • YIELD: 12 SERVINGS, 1 TAQUITO EACH

PER SERVING: 146 CALORIES; 7 G TOTAL FAT; 1 G SATURATED FAT; 4 G PROTEIN; 19 G CARBOHYDRATE; 5 G DIETARY FIBER; 0 MG CHOLESTEROL.

GUY-APPROVED BUFFALO CHICKEN WITH CELERY & GREEK YOGURT DIP

This recipe is one of my buffalo-wing-loving, meat-eating husband's favorites. The celery adds nutrients with very few calories, and yogurt replaces some of the cheese in the dip. It's a perfect choice for game day, casual get-togethers, and cocktail parties.

2 teaspoons (10 ml) extra-virgin olive oil

2 medium celery stalks, diced ⅛ inch, or 3 mm (1½ cups, or 180 g)

3 scallions, thinly sliced, white and green parts, divided

1 tablespoon (9 g) minced garlic

2 (10-ounce, or 280 g) cans chunk chicken breast, drained (3 cups, or 420 g cooked, cubed)

1 cup (250 g) marinara sauce

3 tablespoons (45 ml) hot sauce (use ¼ cup, or 60 ml, to make it spicier)

1 tablespoon (12 g) all-purpose seasoned salt

2 teaspoons (5 g) onion powder

½ teaspoon paprika

¼ teaspoon freshly ground black pepper

½ cup (115 g) light mayonnaise

2 cups (460 g) nonfat plain Greek yogurt

1¼ cups (145 g) shredded reduced fat Cheddar cheese, divided

Whole-grain tortilla chips, carrot and celery sticks for dipping

Heat a large skillet over medium heat and add oil. Add celery, white parts of scallions, and garlic and cook gently for 5 minutes or until tender but not browned. Add chicken, marinara, hot sauce, seasoned salt, onion powder, paprika, and pepper; heat through. Stir in the mayonnaise. Reduce heat to low and add yogurt, 1 cup (115 g) of cheese, and half of the green parts of the scallions.

Pour the dip into a slow cooker set to a low setting and sprinkle remaining ¼ cup (30 g) of cheese on top. Cover and cook until hot, about 40 minutes. Garnish with remaining scallions and serve with chips, carrots, and celery.

 RECIPE NOTE

You can finish heating this dip in a glass dish in the microwave instead of a slow cooker.

TOTAL PREP AND COOK TIME: 1 HOUR • YIELD: 20 SERVINGS, ¼ CUP (30 G) EACH

PER SERVING: 84 CALORIES; 4 G TOTAL FAT; 1 G SATURATED FAT; 9 G PROTEIN; 2 G CARBOHYDRATE; TRACE DIETARY FIBER; 16 MG CHOLESTEROL.

 GO GREEN

While celery is grown year-round, it peaks during winter and summer.

CHICKPEA & OLIVE OIL CRACKERS WITH SESAME SEEDS

Chickpea flour is high in protein and fiber and is a good source of iron. Find it in the natural food section with other flours. Use it to replace some of the flour in baked goods recipes, such as cookies, breads, and cakes, and to thicken soups, sauces, and gravies. Since it's made with 100 percent stone-ground chickpeas, you can also use it in hummus dip and falafel patties. These crackers make a great match for most dips and cheeses.

1¼ cups (150 g) chickpea (garbanzo bean) flour

1¼ cups (150 g) whole-wheat flour

¼ teaspoon salt

¼ teaspoon freshly ground black pepper

⅓ cup + 1 tablespoon (95 ml) extra-virgin olive oil, plus extra for rubbing

4 teaspoons (3 g) chopped thyme (or 1 teaspoon [1 g] dried)

2 tablespoons (16 g) sesame seeds, divided

¼ teaspoon flaked sea or kosher salt

 RECIPE NOTE

If you don't own a sturdy stand mixer, mix the ingredients in a medium bowl and knead the dough by hand.

Place flours, salt, and pepper in the bowl of a stand mixer. Mix with paddle attachment on low until incorporated. Pour in ½ cup + 3 tablespoons (165 ml) of warm water, add oil, and mix on medium speed for 5 to 7 minutes until dough becomes elastic. Add thyme and half of the sesame seeds and mix on low until incorporated. Form dough into a ball and rub lightly with olive oil. Place dough back in bowl, cover it with plastic wrap to prevent it from drying out, and allow it to rest for 30 to 60 minutes.

Preheat oven to 450°F (230°C, or gas mark 8) and line 2 large sheet pans with parchment paper. Divide dough into 2 pieces. Dust work surface and dough with a bit of flour and flatten 1 dough ball with a rolling pin until it is less than ⅛-inch (3 mm) thick (almost paper thin), turning by one-quarter occasionally. Swiftly transfer rolled dough to sheet pan. Repeat with remaining dough. Brush rolled dough lightly with 1 table-spoon (15 ml) of oil and sprinkle remaining sesame seeds and flaked salt on top. Cut in half crosswise with a pizza cutter and separate by 1 inch. Cut into 2½ x 1½-inch (6.4 x 3.8 cm) strips. Bake 16 to 18 minutes until golden and crispy.

TOTAL PREP AND COOK TIME: 45 MINUTES, PLUS RESTING TIME • YIELD: 10 SERVINGS, 5 CRACKERS EACH

PER SERVING: 192 CALORIES; 11 G TOTAL FAT; 1 G SATURATED FAT; 5 G PROTEIN; 20 G CARBOHYDRATE; 5 G DIETARY FIBER; 0 MG CHOLESTEROL.

HEARTY BROCCOLI CHEDDAR & YUKON GOLD POTATO SOUP

There's something about cheesy broccoli soup that evokes my memories of growing up in Wisconsin, the number one cheese-producing state in the United States. But unlike the thick, cream-based recipes of the past, my recipe calls for puréed vegetables, including Yukon Gold potatoes, which lend a silky smooth, buttery taste to the soup. Feel free to substitute a russet potato for the Yukon. You'll think you've gone to heaven when you smell the leeks sautéing on the stovetop.

1 teaspoon (5 ml) expeller-pressed grape-seed or canola oil

1 teaspoon (5 g) butter

1 small onion, thinly sliced (about 1 cup, or 160 g)

1 small leek, halved lengthwise, thinly sliced crosswise, using white and light green parts only (about 1 cup, or 90 g)

1 stalk celery, sliced (about ²/₃ cup, or 80 g)

1 teaspoon (3 g) garlic, sliced

2 Yukon Gold potatoes, peeled, cut into ½-inch (1.3 cm) chunks (about 2 cups, or 220 g)

4 cups (1 L) organic or reduced sodium vegetable broth

1 bay leaf

¼ teaspoon salt

⅛ teaspoon white pepper (or ¼ teaspoon black pepper)

6 cups (426 g) bite-size broccoli florets, divided

1 cup (235 ml) low-fat milk

2 cups (225 g) reduced fat shredded Cheddar cheese, divided

2 cups (112 g) whole-grain croutons or 16 crackers

Heat a large pot over medium heat and add oil and butter. After butter melts and begins to bubble, add onion, leek, celery, and garlic. Sauté until translucent, reducing heat as needed to prevent browning, about 10 minutes. Add potatoes, broth, bay leaf, salt, and pepper, and simmer for 7 minutes. Add 3 cups (213 g) of broccoli and simmer until potatoes and broccoli are fork-tender. Discard bay leaf, add milk, and remove from heat. Ladle soup into a blender and purée for 1 minute until smooth. Add soup back to the pot and add remaining 3 cups (213 g) of broccoli. Simmer for 5 minutes over medium-low until broccoli is tender. Sprinkle in 1½ cups (173 g) of cheese and stir until melted.

Ladle soup into bowls and garnish with remaining ½ cup (58 g) of cheese and croutons. Chill leftovers for up to 3 days.

 GO GREEN

Broccoli is a cool-season crop, peaking in mid-October through December and available year-round in some areas.

TOTAL PREP AND COOK TIME: 45 MINUTES • YIELD: 6 SERVINGS, 1 CUP (235 ML) EACH (WITH ¼ CUP [14 G] CROUTONS AND 1 ROUNDED TABLESPOON [10 G] CHEESE)

PER SERVING: 374 CALORIES; 15 G TOTAL FAT; 5 G SATURATED FAT; 20 G PROTEIN; 42 G CARBOHYDRATE; 7 G DIETARY FIBER; 32 MG CHOLESTEROL.

CREAMY BUTTERNUT SQUASH & APPLE SOUP WITH PEPITAS

This pretty soup has vibrant color and sweet creaminess and is sure to be a hit with your family. I've fed it to the pickiest children and they loved it. You can buy a single can of coconut milk or a carton if you can use it or want to freeze some.

1 tablespoon (15 ml) extra-virgin olive oil

1 carrot, thinly sliced (about 1 cup, or 130 g)

1 small onion, thinly sliced (about 1 cup, or 160 g)

1 gala apple, peeled, thinly sliced (about 1 cup, or 110 g)

1 stalk celery, thinly sliced (about ⅔ cup, or 67 g)

1 small butternut squash, halved lengthwise, seeds scooped, peeled, cubed (about 5 cups, or 700 g)

3½ cups (820 ml) organic or reduced sodium vegetable broth

4 parsley stems

1 bay leaf

½ teaspoon salt

⅛ teaspoon ground white pepper (or ¼ teaspoon freshly ground black pepper)

1 cup (235 ml) light coconut milk (or another type of milk, not fat-free, low-fat okay)

1 teaspoon (5 ml) sherry vinegar (or apple cider vinegar)

¼ cup (35 g) roasted pepitas (hulled pumpkin seeds)

Heat a large pot over medium-high heat and add oil. Add carrot, onion, apple, and celery. Cook gently until tender, gradually reducing heat as needed to prevent browning, about 14 minutes. Add butternut squash, broth, parsley, bay leaf, salt, and pepper, and cover and simmer for 30 minutes until squash is fork-tender. Add milk and vinegar and simmer an additional 5 minutes to reheat.

Remove soup from heat and discard bay leaf and parsley stems. Ladle half of the soup into the blender, cover, and gradually turn up to high speed for 30 seconds or until smooth. Add more broth from the pot if mixture is too thick. Pour soup into another container and purée remaining soup (or pulse for a chunky consistency). Combine puréed soups in the pot and reheat if needed. Pour into serving bowls and garnish with pepitas. Chill leftovers up to 5 days.

RECIPE NOTE

To make peeling winter squash easier, prick thick skins a few times with a sharp fork and microwave 2 to 3 minutes.

TOTAL PREP AND COOK TIME: 45 MINUTES • YIELD: 7 SERVINGS, 1 CUP (235 ML) EACH (WITH 2 TEASPOONS [6 G] PEPITAS)

PER SERVING: 144 CALORIES; 7 G TOTAL FAT; 3 G SATURATED FAT; 4 G PROTEIN; 17 G CARBOHYDRATE; 3 G DIETARY FIBER; 0 MG CHOLESTEROL.

GO GREEN

The best time to enjoy fresh winter squash, including butternut, is during its peak season from October through December. After that, squash have likely been stored for weeks or months.

CHAPTER 3

SPEEDY, SUSTAINABLE SEAFOOD

CAJUN-CRUSTED TILAPIA TACOS WITH PICO DE GALLO

Eating these light and fresh tacos instantly transports me to a coastal beach vacation. I prefer using fresh tilapia for these since it's available year-round and the thickness is a good fit for a small taco. Make a double batch of the pico de gallo for chips and dip!

FOR PICO DE GALLO:

1 large tomato, diced ¼ inch, or 6 mm (1 cup, or 180 g)
⅓ cup (55 g) red onion, diced ¼ inch (6 mm)
2 tablespoons (28 ml) lime juice
2 tablespoons (2 g) chopped cilantro
1 teaspoon (3 g) seeded, deveined, minced jalapeño pepper
½ teaspoon minced garlic
⅛ teaspoon salt
⅛ teaspoon freshly ground black pepper

FOR FISH:

1 pound (455 g) U.S. farm-raised tilapia (or cod, haddock)
¼ cup (60 ml) extra-virgin olive oil, divided
1 teaspoon (3 g) Cajun seasoning (or more for extra kick)
¼ cup (30 g) whole-wheat flour

FOR ASSEMBLY:

8 warm small corn or whole-grain flour tortillas
2 cups (140 g) shredded green cabbage
1 avocado, sliced
4 lime wedges

TO MAKE THE PICO DE GALLO: Place all the pico de gallo ingredients in a small mixing bowl and toss to combine.

TO MAKE THE FISH: Cut tilapia into strips that fit into the size of the tortillas you are using. Heat a large sauté pan over medium-high heat and add 2 tablespoons (28 ml) of oil. Sprinkle Cajun seasoning over fish and dust lightly with flour. When oil is hot and shimmering, add fish to the pan in a single layer, ensuring that pieces are not touching one another. Cook fish in batches, adding 2 tablespoons (28 ml) of oil to each batch as necessary. Cook fish until it is opaque almost halfway through, about 2 minutes. Turn and cook second side until fish is opaque throughout. Remove cooked fish from the pan and place it on a plate lined with paper towels; cover plate with foil to keep warm.

TO ASSEMBLE: Fill tortillas with fish, cabbage, avocado, and pico de gallo. Serve immediately with lime wedge.

 TOTAL PREP AND COOK TIME: 30 MINUTES • YIELD: 4 SERVINGS, 2 TACOS EACH (WITH ¼ CUP [65 G] PICO DE GALLO)

PER SERVING: 473 CALORIES; 25 G TOTAL FAT; 4 G SATURATED FAT; 27 G PROTEIN; 41 G CARBOHYDRATE; 9 G DIETARY FIBER; 45 MG CHOLESTEROL.

 RECIPE NOTE

To save time, you can chop the tomatoes and onion for the pico de gallo in a food processor. Remove and then pulse the jalapeño, cilantro, and garlic together. Combine all of the salsa ingredients in one bowl.

 GO GREEN

If local tomatoes aren't available in your area during winter, use 1 cup (185 g) diced oranges or grapefruit.

 GO CLEAN

When choosing tortillas, look for those that contain the fewest ingredients—ideally just ground corn, lime, and salt in corn tortillas and whole-wheat flour, canola oil, and salt in flour tortillas.

GRILLED CILANTRO SHRIMP TACOS WITH MANGO SALSA

If you don't feel like using the grill, cook the shrimp and marinade in a loosely covered skillet over medium heat, reducing heat as needed. You'll know a mango is ripe when it yields slightly to a gentle squeeze.

FOR SHRIMP:

1 pound (455 g) peeled and deveined large shrimp (21/25 count), tails removed

¼ cup (4 g) chopped cilantro

2 tablespoons (28 ml) lime juice

1 tablespoon (15 ml) expeller-pressed grapeseed or canola oil

2 teaspoons (6 g) minced garlic

¼ teaspoon salt

¼ teaspoon freshly ground black pepper

6 long grill skewers (if using wooden skewers, presoak in water 10 minutes)

FOR SALSA:

1 mango, diced (about 1 cup, or 175 g)

¾ cup (113 g) chopped red bell pepper

2 tablespoons (2 g) chopped cilantro

2 tablespoons (13 g) thinly sliced scallions

2 teaspoons (10 ml) lime juice

½ teaspoon minced garlic

½ teaspoon minced jalapeño (add more to make it spicier)

¼ teaspoon ground cumin

⅛ teaspoon chili powder

1 pinch salt

1 pinch freshly ground black pepper

8 corn or small whole-grain flour tortillas

Extra-virgin olive oil for drizzling

TO MAKE THE SHRIMP: Preheat grill on medium-high heat (400°F, 200°C, or gas mark 6). In a medium bowl, mix shrimp with cilantro, lime juice, oil, garlic, salt, and pepper. Stand 2 skewers up on the counter, ½ inch (1.3 cm) apart with sharp sides pointing up, and thread on the shrimp, pushing them all the way down to 1 inch (2.5 cm) from base of skewers. Repeat until all the shrimp are skewered, being careful to leave small spaces between each. Place shrimp skewers on a sheet pan, cover with plastic wrap, and chill to marinate at least 15 minutes, or up to 4 hours.

TO MAKE THE SALSA: Stir together mango, bell pepper, cilantro, scallions, lime juice, garlic, jalapeño, cumin, chili powder, salt, and pepper.

Oil the grill and place shrimp on the grate. Close the lid and cook for 3 to 4 minutes until shrimp are opaque almost halfway through. Turn skewers over to cook the shrimp through, another 2 to 3 minutes. Remove shrimp from skewers. Heat tortillas on the grill or in a microwave until hot, about 30 seconds. Fill tortillas with shrimp and salsa and drizzle with oil.

TOTAL PREP AND COOK TIME: 1 HOUR, 15 MINUTES • YIELD: 4 SERVINGS, 2 TACOS EACH (WITH 8 SHRIMP AND ⅓ CUP [83 G] SALSA)

PER SERVING: 249 CALORIES; 6 G TOTAL FAT; 1 G SATURATED FAT; 18 G PROTEIN; 32 G CARBOHYDRATE; 5 G DIETARY FIBER; 137 MG CHOLESTEROL.

 RECIPE NOTE

To save time, pulse the salsa ingredients separately in a food processor to chop and then combine in a bowl.

OVEN-FRIED FISH N' CHIPS WITH LEMON YOGURT DIP

While sampling this dish, my assistant Kim announced, "This gives me my pub house fish fry fix!" Just be sure to confirm with the fishmonger that all fish bones have been removed.

FOR CHIPS:
Expeller-pressed canola oil spray
2 medium russet potatoes, cut lengthwise
    into long batons (like French fries)
1 tablespoon (15 ml) expeller-pressed
    grapeseed or canola oil
½ teaspoon Cajun seasoning

FOR FISH:
1 cup (56 g) panko bread crumbs
½ teaspoon Cajun seasoning
1 tablespoon (15 ml) expeller-pressed
    grapeseed or canola oil
3 tablespoons (23 g) whole-wheat flour
1½ teaspoons (4 g) onion powder
½ teaspoon freshly ground black pepper
¼ teaspoon salt
1 large egg
2 teaspoons (10 g) Dijon mustard
1 pound (455 g) cod, cut crosswise into
    $1/3$-inch (1 cm)-thick strips (slightly
    larger than the size of your thumb)

FOR DIP:
¼ cup (60 g) light mayonnaise
¼ cup (60 g) nonfat plain Greek yogurt
1½ teaspoons (8 g) Dijon mustard
1½ teaspoons (8 g) ketchup
1½ teaspoons (8 ml) lemon juice

Arrange 1 rack near the bottom and another in the middle of oven. Preheat oven to 450°F (230°C, or gas mark 8) and line 2 large sheet pans with parchment paper coated with spray.

TO MAKE THE CHIPS: Toss together potatoes, oil, and seasoning on 1 pan and spread out in a single layer. Bake on bottom rack for 45 to 50 minutes, turning chips and rotating pan halfway after 25 minutes, until golden.

TO MAKE THE FISH: Toast bread crumbs in a sauté pan over medium heat for 2 minutes, tossing every 30 seconds until golden. Stir together bread crumbs and Cajun seasoning, drizzling in oil while stirring. In a medium shallow dish, mix flour, onion powder, pepper, and salt. Beat egg, mustard, and 1 teaspoon (5 ml) of water in a third dish. Coat one-third of the fish in the flour mixture, tossing gently with a fork. Lift fish with another fork and add it to egg to coat it. Lift pieces with fork to drain them well and cover them completely with bread crumbs. Arrange pieces of fish in rows on pan, ensuring that they do not touch one another. Bake on middle rack for 10 minutes until fish is white and creamy inside.

TO PREPARE THE DIP: Stir together mayonnaise, yogurt, mustard, ketchup, and lemon juice. Enjoy cooked fish and potatoes immediately with dip. Leftovers can be reheated in the oven at 350°F (180°C, or gas mark 4) the same or the next day.

 GO CLEAN

If you can find it, choose U.S. Pacific, U.S. Alaskan, Icelandic, or northeast Arctic cod (marketed as scrod or whitefish) since these fisheries are well managed and use catching methods with low levels of bycatch that don't damage marine habitats.

TOTAL PREP AND COOK TIME: 60 MINUTES • YIELD: 5 SERVINGS, 3 TO 4 PIECES FISH EACH (WITH ABOUT 12 FRIES AND 1 TABLESPOON [15 G] DIP)

PER SERVING: 382 CALORIES; 10 G TOTAL FAT; 1 G SATURATED FAT; 24 G PROTEIN; 47 G CARBOHYDRATE; 7 G DIETARY FIBER; 82 MG CHOLESTEROL.

SPINACH PARMESAN STUFFED SALMON

You can make these salmon pockets earlier in the day. Allow them to sit on the counter for 30 minutes prior to baking to aid with even cooking. Pop them in the oven for a meal in minutes; they are great when paired with rice pilaf. Feel free to play around with different flavor combinations, such as substituting arugula for spinach or chopped walnuts for pine nuts, and sprinkling on fresh herbs.

Olive oil spray

2 cups (60 g) finely chopped baby spinach (or [40 g] baby arugula)

3 tablespoons (42 g) light mayonnaise

2 tablespoons (14 g) whole-wheat bread crumbs

1 tablespoon (5 g) grated Parmesan cheese

2 teaspoons (10 g) Dijon mustard

¼ teaspoon + 1 pinch freshly ground black pepper

⅛ teaspoon salt

1 pound (455 g) thick, center-cut, skin-on salmon fillets*, cut into 4 portions

Preheat oven to 350°F (180°C, or gas mark 4). Line a sheet pan with parchment paper coated with spray. Combine spinach, mayonnaise, bread crumbs, Parmesan cheese, mustard, pepper, and salt in a bowl. Place the salmon fillets on the sheet pan, folding thin edges underneath themselves to prevent overcooking. Cut lengthwise slits into the salmon, not cutting completely through. Stuff the spinach mixture into the center and mound some onto the top of each fillet. Bake for 17 minutes until the center of the fillet is cooked through.

 TOTAL PREP AND COOK TIME: 30 MINUTES • YIELD: 4 SERVINGS, 1 POCKET EACH

PER SERVING: 217 CALORIES; 13 G TOTAL FAT; 3 G SATURATED FAT; 19 G PROTEIN; 3 G CARBOHYDRATE; 1 G DIETARY FIBER; 51 MG CHOLESTEROL.

 RECIPE NOTE

*Remove the skins if only thin salmon fillets are available. With skinned sides up, place the filling in the centers of the pieces and fold them over like taco shells.

"READY WHEN YOU ARE" HALIBUT & SUMMER SQUASH PAPER POUCHES

You can prepare these pouches earlier in the day or the night before and refrigerate until dinnertime. If you assemble them ahead of time, allow them to sit on the counter for 30 minutes before baking to help ensure even cooking. This dish is elegant enough for company and you can impress your guests by naming it Halibut *en Papillote*, meaning "in paper" in French!

1¼ pounds (570 g) skin-on, boned halibut fillets, cut into 4 portions, blotted dry
¼ teaspoon salt, divided
¼ teaspoon freshly ground black pepper, divided
1 cup (120 g) ¼-inch (6 mm)-diced zucchini
1 cup (120 g) ¼-inch (6 mm)-diced yellow squash
1 cup (150 g) halved cherry tomatoes
¼ cup (40 g) thinly sliced red onion
4 teaspoons (20 ml) extra-virgin olive oil
2 teaspoons (6 g) capers, chopped
2 teaspoons (4 g) grated lemon zest
1 teaspoon (3 g) minced garlic
4 lemon wedges

Preheat oven to 400°F (200°C, or gas mark 6). Season fish with half of the salt and pepper. In a medium bowl, mix zucchini, squash, tomatoes, onion, oil, capers, lemon zest, garlic, and remaining salt and pepper.

Tear off four 15 x 12-inch (38 x 30 cm) sheets of parchment paper; arrange sheets vertically and place fish just below the center on each sheet. Place a heaping ½ cup (60 g) of vegetables on top of each piece of fish. Fold paper over to make the top and bottom corners meet. Beginning with the left corner, fold up 1 inch (2.5 cm), overlapping sections to seal in the contents, and ending with the right corner. Fold each corner under. Finished pouches should look like half-moons. Repeat with remaining pouches and place on a large sheet pan. Bake for 13 minutes for 1-inch (2.5 cm)-thick fillets or until pouches make a strong sizzling sound. Adjust cooking time by a couple of minutes for thinner or thicker fillets.

Remove from the oven and serve immediately, placing pouches on plates or shallow bowls, allowing guests to carefully unwrap or cut into their own portion, avoiding direct contact with hot steam. Serve with lemon wedges.

 GO CLEAN

Pacific halibut (market name Alaskan halibut) caught in Alaska and Canada is the most eco-friendly choice and is lower in mercury and PCBs (polychlorinated biphenyls) than California halibut. Avoid Atlantic halibut, which are so overfished they are off-limits for commercial fishing. Fresh Alaskan halibut peaks in supply and dips in price in May and June. Frozen halibut, including steaks, work beautifully in this recipe, too, as does cod or haddock.

TOTAL PREP AND COOK TIME: 45 MINUTES • YIELD: 4 SERVINGS, 1 POUCH EACH

PER SERVING: 228 CALORIES; 8 G TOTAL FAT; 1 G SATURATED FAT; 31 G PROTEIN; 8 G CARBOHYDRATE; 2 G DIETARY FIBER; 46 MG CHOLESTEROL.

PISTACHIO & WHOLE-GRAIN TORTILLA CRUSTED TILAPIA WITH CHILI LIME SAUCE

A clean-eating mantra includes wasting as little food as possible. This recipe provides an excellent vehicle for using up the small, broken tortilla chips at the bottom of the bag. To chop the chips and nuts quickly, try smashing them in a reusable plastic bag with a mallet or rolling pin, or whir them in a food processor.

FOR TILAPIA:

1 large egg
¼ cup (4 g) finely chopped cilantro
1 teaspoon Dijon mustard
½ cup (60 g) crushed whole-grain tortilla chips (from about 12 large whole chips)
¼ cup (31 g) finely chopped pistachios
1 teaspoon (13 g) ground cumin
½ teaspoon garlic powder
¼ teaspoon chili powder
¼ teaspoon salt
¼ teaspoon freshly ground black pepper
1 pound (455 g) tilapia fillets, cut into at least 4 portions (or cod, haddock)

FOR SAUCE:

¼ cup (60 g) light mayonnaise
1 teaspoon (5 ml) lime juice
1 pinch chili powder
1 pinch salt

TO MAKE THE TILAPIA: Preheat oven to 425°F (220°C, or gas mark 7). Line a large sheet pan with parchment paper or a silicone baking mat. Whisk egg, cilantro, mustard, and 1 teaspoon (5 ml) of water together in a shallow dish. In another dish, combine chips, pistachios, cumin, garlic powder, chili powder, salt, and pepper. Dip fish in egg mixture, coating on both sides, and then coat fish well in breading. Place fish on pan with rounded side up. Bake for 14 minutes until golden on the outside and opaque and slightly firm in the center.

TO MAKE THE SAUCE: Blend all sauce ingredients.

Serve the fish immediately with the sauce.

GO CLEAN

» Choose U.S. farm-raised tilapia, which is low in contaminants and is produced with eco-friendlier practices than those of Southeast Asia and Latin America.

» Besides being green in color, pistachios are green for the environment. Approximately 1 ounce (28 g) of pistachios provides about the same amount of protein as 1 ounce (28 g) of raw red meat, using only a tiny fraction of the fossil fuel required to produce it. For a smaller carbon footprint, look for pistachios originating closer to home, instead of those from across the globe.

TOTAL PREP AND COOK TIME: 40 MINUTES • YIELD: 4 SERVINGS, 1 LARGE OR 2 SMALL PIECES OF TILAPIA EACH (WITH 1 TABLESPOON [15 G] OF SAUCE)

PER SERVING: 264 CALORIES; 18 G TOTAL FAT; 2 G SATURATED FAT; 25 G PROTEIN; 12 G CARBOHYDRATE; 2 G DIETARY FIBER; 97 MG CHOLESTEROL.

SIZZLING SICHUAN SHRIMP & STRING BEAN STIR-FRY

This recipe offers a way to use green beans in a main course, another option for peak season when beans are so abundant. Black bean sauce lasts awhile in the refrigerator, so you'll be able to use it over time in stir-fries.

FOR SAUCE:

2 tablespoons (30 g) black bean sauce (found in Asian food section)

2 tablespoons (28 ml) rice wine (or mirin, vermouth, or dry sherry)

2 tablespoons (28 ml) reduced sodium soy sauce

2 teaspoons (13 g) honey

FOR STIR-FRY:

4 teaspoons (20 ml) expeller-pressed grapeseed or canola oil, divided

1 pound (455 g) green beans, trimmed and dried completely

1 pound (455 g) peeled and deveined large shrimp (21/25 count), tails removed

3 dried red chiles, more or less to adjust spiciness

1 scallion, chopped

1 tablespoon (10 g) minced garlic

1 tablespoon (6 g) minced ginger

1 teaspoon (5 ml) reduced sodium soy sauce

4 cups (780 g) cooked brown rice (or rice noodles)

TO MAKE THE SAUCE: Blend all the sauce ingredients in a small bowl with 2 tablespoons (28 ml) of water.

TO MAKE THE STIR-FRY: Heat a wok or a large pot over medium heat and add oil. When oil is shimmering, add beans and cook until slightly wrinkled, stir-frying every 60 seconds, about 5 minutes. Place beans on a plate. Put the wok back on the heat, add shrimp, chiles, scallions, garlic, ginger and 1 teaspoon (5 ml) soy sauce, and cook just until shrimp are opaque in the center, about 3 minutes. Remove chiles and swirl in the sauce. Add beans to reheat, mixing well. Serve over rice.

 GO CLEAN

Only 2 percent of imported shrimp from China, Malaysia, India, and Vietnam are tested by the U.S. Food and Drug Administration (FDA) to monitor illegal antibiotic and pesticide content. The FDA tests for thirteen types of drug residues, while Europe and Japan test for more than twice that amount. Much of this imported shrimp is also produced with child and forced labor, providing one more reason to choose local foods. The eco-friendliest shrimp of this size include U.S. farmed and British Columbian wild-caught, with U.S. wild-caught being a good alternative. Avoid farmed shrimp from Mexico and imported wild-caught shrimp.

 TOTAL PREP AND COOK TIME: 30 MINUTES • YIELD: 4 SERVINGS, 1 CUP (232 G) STIR-FRY EACH (WITH 1 CUP [195 G] RICE)

PER SERVING: 394 CALORIES; 8 G TOTAL FAT; 1 G SATURATED FAT; 23 G PROTEIN; 59 G CARBOHYDRATE; 7 G DIETARY FIBER; 137 MG CHOLESTEROL.

ALMOND & DILL CRUSTED BARRAMUNDI FILLETS

Barramundi (think snapper crossed with halibut) is the next big thing in seafood because it contains more than twice the amount of healthy omega-3 fish oils as tilapia and undetectable levels of mercury, antibiotics, hormones, PCBs (polychlorinated biphenyls), and other contaminants found in other fish. Find it in the freezer section of major retailers or substitute tilapia in this recipe.

FOR BARRAMUNDI:

⅓ cup (77 g) nonfat plain Greek yogurt
3 tablespoons (12 g) chopped dill
   (or 1 teaspoon [1 g] dried dill)
2 teaspoons (8 g) Dijon mustard
⅓ cup (38 g) whole-wheat bread crumbs
¼ cup (28 g) sliced almonds
¼ cup (25 g) grated Parmesan cheese
¼ teaspoon onion powder
¼ teaspoon salt
¼ teaspoon freshly ground black pepper
1 pound (455 g) frozen barramundi fillets,
   thawed, blotted dry, cut into 4 portions
4 lemon wedges

FOR SAUCE:

¼ cup (60 g) nonfat plain Greek yogurt
2 tablespoons (28 g) light mayonnaise
1 teaspoon (3 g) capers, chopped
1 teaspoon (5 ml) lemon juice
⅛ teaspoon garlic powder
⅛ teaspoon salt

TO MAKE THE BARRAMUNDI: Preheat oven to 425°F (220°C, or gas mark 7). Line a large sheet pan with parchment paper or a silicone baking mat. Stir yogurt, dill, and mustard together in a shallow dish. In another dish, combine bread crumbs, almonds, Parmesan cheese, onion powder, salt, and pepper.

Dip fish in yogurt, coating both sides, and then coat fish well in breading. Place fish on pan with rounded side of fish facing up. Bake for 15 to 20 minutes, turning fish after 10 minutes, until golden on the outside and opaque and slightly firm in the center.

TO MAKE THE SAUCE: Blend all the sauce ingredients.

Serve the fish immediately with the sauce and lemon wedges on the side.

 GO CLEAN

Leading environmental groups recognize farm-raised barramundi for its land-based farming systems, considered "the gold standard" for sustainable aquaculture, and mostly vegetarian diet. Central Vietnam also produces sustainable barramundi in a clean, nonpolluted bay.

 TOTAL PREP AND COOK TIME: 30 MINUTES • YIELD: 4 SERVINGS, 1 PIECE EACH (WITH 1 ROUNDED TABLESPOON [15 G] SAUCE)

PER SERVING: 215 CALORIES; 8 G TOTAL FAT; 1 G SATURATED FAT; 25 G PROTEIN; 12 G CARBOHYDRATE; 2 G DIETARY FIBER; 43 MG CHOLESTEROL.

TOASTED SESAME SALMON NUGGETS WITH SWEET-SAVORY SCALLION SAUCE

Scarlet devoured wild Alaskan salmon as a baby, until her finicky eating habits kicked in at age two. At two-and-a-half years old she tried these nuggets with natural ketchup and gobbled them up, thinking they were chicken!

FOR NUGGETS:

1 cup (56 g) panko bread crumbs

3 tablespoons (22 g) whole-wheat flour

1½ teaspoons (4.5 g) garlic powder

¼ teaspoon salt

¼ teaspoon freshly ground black pepper

1 tablespoon (8 g) black sesame seeds

½ teaspoon Chinese 5-spice powder (or
  ¼ teaspoon cinnamon and ⅛ teaspoon
  each ground fennel and cloves)

1 tablespoon (15 ml) expeller-pressed
  grapeseed or canola oil

1 large egg

2 teaspoons (8 g) Chinese mustard

1 teaspoon (5 ml) reduced sodium soy
  sauce

1 pound (455 g) skinned salmon, cut
  crosswise into ½ x 2-inch (1.3 x 5 cm)
  strips

FOR SAUCE:

2 tablespoons (12 g) thinly sliced scallions

4 teaspoons (27 g) sweet chili sauce
  (found in Asian food section)

2 teaspoons (10 ml) reduced sodium soy
  sauce

2 teaspoons (8 g) Chinese mustard

TO MAKE THE NUGGETS: Preheat oven to 450°F (230°C, or gas mark 8) and line a large sheet pan with parchment paper. Toast bread crumbs in a sauté pan over medium heat for 2 minutes, tossing every 30 seconds until golden. Mix flour, garlic powder, salt, and pepper in a medium shallow dish. In another dish, stir together toasted bread crumbs, sesame seeds, and 5-spice powder, drizzling in oil while stirring. Beat egg, mustard, and soy sauce in a third dish. Coat one-third of the batch of fish in the flour mixture, tossing gently with a fork. Lift the fish with another fork and coat it with the egg mixture. Lift the pieces with a fork to drain them and cover them completely with the bread crumbs. Arrange them closely, but not touching, in rows on the pan. Bake on middle rack for 10 minutes until fish is creamy inside and slightly firm.

TO PREPARE THE SAUCE: Stir together all sauce ingredients. Enjoy the fish immediately with the sauce. Leftovers can be reheated in the oven at 350°F (180°C, or gas mark 4) until heated through, the same or the next day.

GO CLEAN

Choose fresh wild Alaskan salmon during peak season (April through October), which is superior in sustainability and taste. Wild salmon from Washington and British Columbia rank second. Avoid Atlantic farm-raised salmon, which contains high levels of PCBs (polychlorinated biphenyls), a toxic industrial chemical that is banned in the United States and lingers in bodies of water.

TOTAL PREP AND COOK TIME: 45 MINUTES • YIELD: 5 SERVINGS, 3 TO 4 NUGGETS EACH (WITH 1 TABLESPOON [15 G] SAUCE)

PER SERVING: 253 CALORIES; 13 G TOTAL FAT; 2 G SATURATED FAT; 18 G PROTEIN; 15 G CARBOHYDRATE; 1 G DIETARY FIBER; 82 MG CHOLESTEROL.

PAN ROASTED TROUT WITH WARM TOMATO CAPER SALAD

Feel free to substitute salmon or tilapia for the trout, increasing cooking time as needed for thicker fillets.

2 whole, skin-on, rainbow trout fillets (about 1 pound, or 455 g)

¼ teaspoon salt

¼ teaspoon freshly ground black pepper

⅛ teaspoon garlic powder

2 teaspoons (10 ml) expeller-pressed grapeseed or canola oil

2 tablespoons (20 g) minced shallot or red onion

2 cups (300 g) halved cherry tomatoes

¼ cup (25 g) pitted kalamata olives, halved

1 teaspoon (3 g) capers, chopped

¼ cup (15 g) chopped Italian flat-leaf parsley

Season the skinless side of the trout with salt, pepper, and garlic powder. Fold the trout back into the shape of a whole fish. Heat a large frying pan over medium-high heat and add oil. When oil begins to shimmer, place trout in the pan.* Tilt the pan slightly to evenly coat the bottom of the fish with oil. Reduce heat to medium and cook for 5 minutes or until trout is browned on one side and opaque almost halfway through. Turn and cook for 5 minutes until all flesh is opaque and top center (the thickest part) yields to gentle pressure, but before it is completely firm. Place trout on a plate near the stovetop to keep it warm.

Return pan to heat set to medium-low, add shallots, and cook until translucent, about 1 minute. Add tomatoes, olives, and capers. Sauté until tomatoes have softened a bit, about 2 minutes. Stir in parsley and remove from heat. Reopen the trout and divide into 4 servings. Spoon on tomato topping and serve immediately.

 GO CLEAN

Farm-raised rainbow trout, otherwise marketed as golden or steelhead trout, ranks well in sustainability and omega-3 content. It looks like and tastes milder than salmon, and works beautifully here. Avoid Lake Michigan trout, which is over-fished and in serious decline.

 RECIPE NOTES

» *If using steelhead trout, which is thicker than other varieties, cut it into individual portions, cooking skin-less side first, about 4 minutes, and 2 to 3 minutes on the other side.

» You can omit the olives and capers and add 1 teaspoon (5 ml) of lemon juice or balsamic vinegar and a bit of extra salt in its place.

 TOTAL PREP AND COOK TIME: 20 MINUTES • YIELD: 4 SERVINGS, 1 PIECE FISH EACH (WITH ½ CUP [90 G] TOMATO TOPPING)

PER SERVING: 198 CALORIES; 10 G TOTAL FAT; 1 G SATURATED FAT; 22 G PROTEIN; 4 G CARBOHYDRATE; 1 G DIETARY FIBER; 59 MG CHOLESTEROL.

ANGEL HAIR PASTA WITH SHRIMP, SUMMER VEGETABLES & FRESH GOAT CHEESE

This recipe offers an exciting change from red sauced pasta dishes. The goat cheese melts and clings to the pasta, tricking your taste buds into thinking it's a cream-based sauce.

2 tablespoons (28 ml) extra-virgin olive oil, divided

½ cup (80 g) diced red onion

2 teaspoons (6 g) minced garlic

1 medium zucchini, sliced into half-moons (about 1¾ cups, or 210 g)

1 medium yellow summer squash, sliced into half-moons or quarters (about 2 cups, or 240 g)

½ teaspoon dried oregano (or use 2 tablespoons [8 g] fresh, chopped to stir in at the end)

½ teaspoon dried basil (or use 2 tablespoons [5 g] fresh; see Recipe Note)

¼ teaspoon salt

¼ teaspoon freshly ground black pepper

1¼ pounds (570 g) peeled and deveined large shrimp (21/25 count), tails removed

¼ cup (60 ml) dry white wine or vegetable broth

2 cups (40 g) lightly packed arugula (or [60 g] baby spinach)

1 cup (150 g) halved cherry tomatoes

3 cups (420 g) cooked whole-grain angel hair pasta

⅓ cup (90 g) soft goat cheese

2 tablespoons (28 ml) lemon juice

¼ cup (25 g) grated Parmesan cheese

Heat a large skillet over medium-low heat and pour in 1 tablespoon (15 ml) of oil. When oil is shimmering, add onion and garlic and cook until translucent, about 4 minutes, reducing heat as needed. Add zucchini, squash, oregano, basil, salt, and pepper and cook for 6 minutes until tender. Add shrimp and wine; cover with a lid left slightly ajar and cook until almost done, about 4 minutes. Add arugula and tomatoes and cook until wilted and shrimp is cooked through, about 2 minutes. Add cooked pasta and reheat.

Remove from heat and add the pieces of goat cheese; stir until melted and toss with remaining tablespoon (15 ml) of oil and lemon juice. Garnish with Parmesan cheese and serve hot.

 RECIPE NOTE

For the dried basil, you can substitute in 2 tablespoons (5 g) of fresh basil cut in a chiffonade by stacking the basil leaves, rolling them lengthwise, slicing them very thin crosswise, and sprinkling them in at the end of the cooking process.

 GO GREEN

Summer squash, including zucchini and three varieties of yellow squash, is a moderately warm-season crop and peaks during late spring, summer, and early fall depending on the region.

 TOTAL PREP AND COOK TIME: 30 MINUTES • YIELD: 4 SERVINGS, 1½ CUPS (APPROX. 476 G) EACH

PER SERVING: 447 CALORIES; 16 G TOTAL FAT; 5 G SATURATED FAT; 34 G PROTEIN; 41 G CARBOHYDRATE; 6 G DIETARY FIBER; 193 MG CHOLESTEROL.

LEAN & GREEN DILL SALMON BURGERS WITH CREAMY COCKTAIL SAUCE

Making these from scratch instead of buying frozen patties results in a more moist, fresher burger. This is a great recipe for using frozen wild Alaskan salmon, if fresh is out of season. Ask the fishmonger to remove the skin from fresh salmon to save you the hassle.

FOR BURGERS:

1¼ pounds (570 g) wild Alaskan salmon, skinned, boned, cut into 6 large chunks
¼ cup (16 g) stemmed fresh dill (or 4 teaspoons [4 g] dried dill)
1 scallion, cut into 4 pieces
2 teaspoons (10 g) Dijon mustard
2 teaspoons (10 ml) sherry vinegar (or red wine vinegar or rice vinegar)
2 teaspoons (10 ml) reduced sodium soy sauce
1 small garlic clove
¼ teaspoon freshly ground black pepper
Expeller-pressed canola oil spray
4 whole-grain hamburger buns
1 avocado, thinly sliced
8 slices tomato
1 cup (55 g) leafy salad greens
Lemon wedges

FOR SAUCE:

3 tablespoons (42 g) olive oil mayonnaise
4½ teaspoons (27 g) cocktail sauce

TO MAKE THE BURGERS: Preheat grill on medium heat, 375°F (190°C, or gas mark 5). Add 3 pieces of salmon, along with dill, scallion, mustard, vinegar, soy sauce, garlic, and pepper, to a food processor and run until mixture becomes pasty. Scrape down the sides of the bowl and add remaining salmon. Pulse a few times until chunks become bite-size pieces. Gently form salmon into 4 patties, not overworking, to make a tender burger. Lightly coat the cut sides of buns with spray. Oil the grill and place burgers on grate; cook for 4 minutes on the first side and 2 minutes on the flip side. Place cut side of buns on the grill to toast, right after flipping the burgers. Remove patties and buns from grill.

TO MAKE THE SAUCE: Blend mayonnaise and cocktail sauce in a small bowl. Serve each patty on a bun with avocado, tomato, salad greens, lemon wedges, and sauce.

 GO GREEN

Dill season peaks in summer and early fall. Substitute Italian flat-leaf parsley when or if fresh dill isn't available.

 RECIPE NOTES

» You can make your own cocktail sauce with 1 tablespoon (15 g) of natural ketchup, 1 teaspoon of horseradish (or more or less to taste), and ½ teaspoon of lemon juice.

» If you don't feel like grilling, sauté the patties in 2 teaspoons (10 ml) of olive oil (or lightly sprayed) in a large frying pan over medium heat.

 TOTAL PREP AND COOK TIME: 30 MINUTES • YIELD: 4 SERVINGS, 1 BURGER EACH (WITH ¼ AVOCADO, 2 TOMATO SLICES, ¼ CUP [14 G] GREENS, AND 1 TABLESPOON [15 G] SAUCE)

PER SERVING: 536 CALORIES; 26 G TOTAL FAT; 4 G SATURATED FAT; 33 G PROTEIN; 43 G CARBOHYDRATE; 10 G DIETARY FIBER; 66 MG CHOLESTEROL.

ONE-POT SHRIMP PAD THAI WITH CARROTS & BEAN SPROUTS

When you're looking for an "out of the ordinary" dish to wake up your taste buds, this recipe really hits the spot. I add shredded carrots and extra bean sprouts, which turns this dish into an all-in-one meal.

1 (8-ounce, or 225 g) package wide (like fettuccine) Thai brown rice noodles

FOR SAUCE:
3 tablespoons (45 ml) rice vinegar or white distilled vinegar
2 tablespoons (40 g) light agave nectar
2 tablespoons (28 ml) lime juice
4 teaspoons (20 ml) fish sauce (or reduced sodium soy sauce for a milder flavor)
1 teaspoon (5 ml) Worcestershire sauce

TO MIX WITH THE NOODLES:
2 tablespoons (28 ml) expeller-pressed grapeseed or canola oil
1 pound (455 g) peeled and deveined large shrimp (21/25 count), tails removed
1 tablespoon (9 g) minced garlic
1 large shallot, minced (about ⅓ cup, or 53 g)
1½ cups (130 g) matchstick-cut carrots
½ cup (25 g) ½-inch (1.3 cm)-sliced scallions, white and green parts, divided
1 tablespoon (15 ml) fish sauce
1 large egg
2 cups (208 g) bean sprouts (from mung beans), divided
⅓ cup (48 g) unsalted, dry-roasted peanuts, finely chopped
⅛ teaspoon white pepper
4 lime wedges

Soak noodles in water that is lukewarm or room temperature until flexible, not completely soft or mushy, about 45 minutes.

TO MAKE THE SAUCE: Mix together sauce ingredients and drain the noodles.

TO MAKE THE NOODLES: Heat a large wok or pot over high heat and add oil. Add shrimp, garlic, shallots, carrots, white parts of scallions, and fish sauce to the wok and cook for 4 minutes until vegetables are tender. Add noodles to vegetable mixture, stir-frying vigorously to prevent sticking. Stir in sauce. Turn up the heat to evaporate the liquid if you have excess liquid remaining on the bottom of the wok. Push noodles to one side of the wok; add egg to the other side and scramble. Incorporate the egg, green parts of scallions, and half of the bean sprouts into the noodles. Taste a noodle, and if it's too hard, add a little water to the pan. Finished noodles should be soft, dry, and tangled. Stir in peanuts and pepper. Serve hot with remaining bean sprouts and lime.

 GO CLEAN

"Go organic" with whole peanuts and peanut butter since conventionally grown peanuts have higher pesticide residues. Any peanuts are highly susceptible to aflatoxin, a mold linked to liver cancer. Contamination is most common in areas with hot, damp climates and poor storage facilities, is generally low in Europe, but occasionally is high in the United States. To limit exposure to aflatoxin, choose the freshest peanuts available and refrigerate up to several months.

TOTAL PREP AND COOK TIME: 40 MINUTES, PLUS SOAKING TIME • YIELD: 4 SERVINGS, 1½ CUPS (APPROX. 252 G) EACH (WITH ¼ CUP [26 G] SPROUTS)

PER SERVING: 505 CALORIES; 14 G TOTAL FAT; 2 G SATURATED FAT; 24 G PROTEIN; 70 G CARBOHYDRATE; 5 G DIETARY FIBER; 191 MG CHOLESTEROL.

CHAPTER 4

PROTEIN-PACKED POULTRY & MEAT MAINS

SKINNY CHICKEN PARMESAN WITH SPINACH

When I was a private chef, my employer requested a healthier version of chicken Parmesan. This recipe became one of my signature dishes and a favorite of the house.

Olive oil spray

FOR SAUCE:

2 teaspoons (10 ml) extra-virgin olive oil

2 cloves garlic, sliced

1 (28-ounce, or 785 g) can whole
   tomatoes

¼ teaspoon dried basil

¼ teaspoon dried oregano

2 pinches salt

2 pinches freshly ground black pepper

½ teaspoon honey

FOR CHICKEN:

3 tablespoons (15 g) grated Parmesan
   cheese

2 tablespoons (16 g) whole-wheat flour

½ teaspoon salt, divided

¼ teaspoon freshly ground black pepper

¼ teaspoon dried basil

1½ pounds (680 g) chicken breast,
   cut into 6 pieces, pounded to ¼ inch
   (6 mm)

2 tablespoons + 2 teaspoons (38 ml)
   extra-virgin olive oil, divided

4 cups (120 g) baby spinach

1 teaspoon (5 ml) lemon juice

¾ cup (86 g) fresh mozzarella cheese,
   sliced into 6 medallions (or shredded)

6 cups (840 g) cooked whole-grain thin
   spaghetti tossed in 2 teaspoons (10 ml)
   olive oil

Preheat oven to 375°F (190°C, or gas mark 5) and coat the bottom of a 9 x 13-inch (23 x 33 cm) pan with olive oil spray.

TO MAKE THE SAUCE: Heat a medium saucepan over medium heat. Add oil and garlic and cook gently for 30 seconds. Do not brown. With your hand, squeeze each tomato into the pan and add basil, oregano, salt, pepper, and honey. Reduce to medium heat and simmer for 20 minutes, lowering the heat as needed.

TO MAKE THE CHICKEN: Combine Parmesan cheese, flour, salt, pepper, and basil in a medium dish and coat chicken with cheese mixture. Place a large skillet over medium heat and add 2 tablespoons (28 ml) of oil. When oil is shimmering, add chicken, rounded-side down, and cook until golden on one side, about 5 minutes. Arrange chicken in a baking pan. Pour remaining 2 teaspoons (10 ml) of oil into skillet and add spinach. Cook spinach for 1 to 2 minutes until wilted and swirl in lemon juice. Gently press spinach to release water and divide spinach on top of chicken. Spoon sauce around and over the chicken, place mozzarella on top, and sprinkle with ¼ teaspoon salt. Bake for 15 minutes until chicken is cooked through. Serve over spaghetti.

 GO GREEN

Spinach is a cool-season crop and peaks during the months of September and October. Warmer climates may produce spinach year-round, but yield may dip in December and January.

TOTAL PREP AND COOK TIME: 55 MINUTES • YIELD: 6 SERVINGS, 1 PIECE CHICKEN EACH (WITH ¼ CUP [62 G] SAUCE AND 1 CUP [140 G] SPAGHETTI)

PER SERVING: 452 CALORIES; 14 G TOTAL FAT; 4 G SATURATED FAT; 38 G PROTEIN; 42 G CARBOHYDRATE; 4 G DIETARY FIBER; 80 MG CHOLESTEROL.

TURKEY & OAT MEATBALLS WITH TOMATO & CARROT MARINARA SAUCE

Kimberly, one of my BFFs, loved this dish when I made it for her and our kids, and she couldn't wait to get her hands on the recipe. Ask and you shall receive!

FOR SAUCE:

1 tablespoon (15 ml) extra-virgin olive oil

1 cup (160 g) diced onion

2 teaspoons (6 g) minced garlic

3 tablespoons (48 g) tomato paste

1 (28-ounce, or 785 g) can whole
   tomatoes

¾ cup (83 g) finely shredded carrots

1 tablespoon (15 ml) red wine vinegar

1 teaspoon (7 g) honey

1 teaspoon (2 g) Italian herb seasoning

½ teaspoon salt

¼ teaspoon freshly ground black pepper

FOR MEATBALLS:

3 tablespoons (45 ml) low-fat milk

⅓ cup (27 g) dry oats, pulverized in food
   processor or with immersion blender

1 pound (455 g) lean ground turkey

1 cup (160 g) finely diced onion

¼ cup (25 g) grated Parmesan cheese

1 large egg

2 tablespoons (12 g) Italian herb
   seasoning

1 tablespoon (10 g) minced garlic

1 tablespoon (15 ml) red wine vinegar

½ teaspoon salt

¼ teaspoon fennel seed, pulverized in
   mortar and pestle or pounded in
   plastic bag

4 tablespoons (60 ml) extra-virgin olive oil,
   divided

6 cups (840 g) cooked whole-grain thin
   spaghetti tossed in 1 tablespoon
   (15 ml) extra-virgin olive oil

TO MAKE THE SAUCE: Heat a large pot over medium heat and add oil. Add onion and garlic and sauté until translucent. Add tomato paste and brown slightly, stirring occasionally, about 3 to 5 minutes. Using your hand, squeeze tomatoes over a bowl, discarding seeds, and add tomatoes to pot. Stir in remaining tomato juice from the can, along with carrots, vinegar, honey, Italian seasoning, salt, and pepper. Simmer for 20 minutes.

TO MAKE THE MEATBALLS: Stir milk and oats together in a large bowl. Add turkey and remaining ingredients, except oil and spaghetti, and blend well. Roll into bite-size balls. Heat a large skillet over medium heat and add 2 tablespoons (28 ml) oil. When the oil is shimmering, add meatballs in a single layer and brown them on all sides. Add the meatballs to the sauce. Repeat with remaining oil and meatballs. Serve the meatballs and sauce on top of the spaghetti.

 RECIPE NOTE

Regular ground turkey contains the skin, bringing the saturated fat content as high as regular ground beef. Buy "lean" for the perfect proportion of protein, fat, and flavor without the taste sacrifice of "extra-lean."

TOTAL PREP AND COOK TIME: 55 MINUTES • YIELD: 6 SERVINGS, 4 MEATBALLS COATED WITH SAUCE EACH (WITH 1 CUP [140 G] PASTA)

PER SERVING: 394 CALORIES; 9 G TOTAL FAT; 2 G SATURATED FAT; 23 G PROTEIN; 56 G CARBOHYDRATE; 5 G DIETARY FIBER; 59 MG CHOLESTEROL.

SESAME CHICKEN STIR-FRY WITH SNOW PEAS & CARROTS

This rice bowl dish serves as an excellent beginner stir-fry and has a mildly pleasant flavor to suit the taste preferences of all ages. Scarlet devours the thin strips of chicken along with spoonfuls of rice. One serving provides a meal in itself with plenty of vegetables, lean protein, and whole grains.

FOR CHICKEN:

1 large egg white
2 teaspoons (5 g) cornstarch
½ teaspoon salt
1 pound (455 g) chicken breast, cut into thin 2-inch (5 cm)-long strips
1 tablespoon (15 ml) expeller-pressed grapeseed or canola oil

FOR SAUCE:

2 tablespoons (28 ml) rice wine (or dry sherry or vermouth)
2 scallions, sliced
1 tablespoon (15 ml) cider vinegar
1 tablespoon (15 ml) reduced sodium soy sauce
2 teaspoons (10 g) black bean sauce (in Asian food section)
1 tablespoon (20 g) honey
1 teaspoon (5 ml) dark sesame seed oil
½ teaspoon roasted Sichuan peppercorns, crushed (or coarsely ground black pepper)

FOR VEGETABLES:

1 tablespoon + 1 teaspoon (11 g) sesame seeds
2 teaspoons (10 ml) expeller-pressed grapeseed or canola oil
2 medium carrots, coarsely shredded (1 cup, or 110 g)
1 cup (63 g) snow peas, trimmed, cut diagonally in half (or sugar snap peas)
1 teaspoon (5 ml) reduced sodium soy sauce

FOR SERVING:

3 cups (585 g) cooked brown rice

TO PREPARE THE CHICKEN: Whisk together egg white, cornstarch, and salt in a medium bowl; toss chicken in this mixture to coat it. Chill while preparing the other ingredients.

TO PREPARE THE SAUCE: Stir all the sauce ingredients together in a small bowl.

Heat a large sauté pan or wok over medium-high heat and add 1 tablespoon (15 ml) oil. When oil is shimmering, add chicken in a single layer and brown for 4 minutes, tossing frequently. Place chicken on a plate. Reduce heat to medium-low; add sesame seeds to the same pan and toast for 1 minute until fragrant and golden. Add a splash of water, scraping to loosen brown bits.

TO COOK THE VEGETABLES: Raise the heat to medium-high, swirl 2 teaspoons (10 ml) oil into the pan, add vegetables, and stir-fry for 2 minutes, adding soy sauce halfway through. Add sauce and cook for 30 seconds. Stir in the chicken to reheat.

TO SERVE: Spoon over rice.

 GO GREEN

Edible-pod peas are grown year-round in mildly cool climates and peak in spring, summer, and fall months. You may substitute thawed frozen green peas if domestically grown varieties are unavailable.

 TOTAL PREP AND COOK TIME: 30 MINUTES • YIELD: 4 SERVINGS, 1 CUP (APPROX. 163 G) STIR-FRY EACH (WITH ¾ CUP [146 G] RICE)

PER SERVING: 391 CALORIES; 9 G TOTAL FAT; 1 G SATURATED FAT; 32 G PROTEIN; 43 G CARBOHYDRATE; 5 G DIETARY FIBER; 62 MG CHOLESTEROL.

PECAN-CRUSTED CHICKEN TENDERS WITH YOGURT DILL DIP

I'll admit it. I love to eat breaded, deep-fried chicken strips dipped in creamy ranch dressing, and on rare occasions, I will order them while out running errands all day. I prepare this recipe at home after a decent lapse since my last fix. For ultimate satisfaction, pair with Oven-Fried Chips (page 52).

FOR CHICKEN:

½ cup (55 g) pecans

⅓ cup (40 g) whole-wheat flour

2 teaspoons (5 g) paprika

2 teaspoons (6 g) dry mustard

2 teaspoons (6 g) garlic powder

1 teaspoon (2 g) onion powder

½ teaspoon salt

½ teaspoon freshly ground black pepper

1 tablespoon (15 ml) expeller-pressed canola oil

½ cup (56 g) panko bread crumbs

1 large egg

1 pound (455 g) chicken tenders, larger pieces cut in half lengthwise

FOR DIP:

¼ cup (60 g) nonfat plain Greek yogurt

¼ cup (60 g) light mayonnaise

1 teaspoon (5 ml) lemon juice

¼ teaspoon dried dill

¼ teaspoon garlic powder

¼ teaspoon onion powder

1 pinch salt

1 pinch freshly ground black pepper

TO MAKE THE CHICKEN: Preheat oven to 475°F (240°C, or gas mark 9) and line a sheet pan with parchment paper. Whir pecans, flour, paprika, dry mustard, garlic and onion powder, salt, and pepper in a food processor until pecans are ground to a powder, about 30 seconds. Drizzle in the oil with the motor running, blending completely. Transfer mixture to a shallow dish and stir in the panko bread crumbs.

Beat egg in a second shallow dish and add chicken tenders, coating them completely. Transfer each tender to the breading, turning to coat evenly. Arrange chicken on the prepared pan. Bake until golden brown and nearly firm, 8 minutes.

TO MAKE THE DIP: Stir all the dip ingredients together in a small bowl.

Enjoy the cooked chicken immediately with the dip.

 RECIPE NOTE

Chicken tenders come from the undersides of chicken breasts and are naturally portioned into strips, saving you time in cutting them. If you don't have chicken tenders, substitute chicken breasts cut into 4 x 1-inch (10 x 2.5 cm) strips.

 TOTAL PREP AND COOK TIME: 30 MINUTES • YIELD: 4 SERVINGS, 2 TO 3 TENDERS EACH (WITH 1 TABLESPOON [15 G] DIP)

PER SERVING: 418 CALORIES; 20 G TOTAL FAT; 3 G SATURATED FAT; 34 G PROTEIN; 23 G CARBOHYDRATE; 4 G DIETARY FIBER; 120 MG CHOLESTEROL.

GRILLED BALSAMIC CHICKEN MEDALLIONS WITH TRICOLOR BELL PEPPERS & RED ONION

In the summertime I try to follow three rules for dinners: 1) require minimal effort to prepare, 2) made with light, garden-fresh ingredients, and 3) grilled instead of cooked in a hot oven. This recipe meets all three requirements. Serve it with a whole-grain baguette, sliced, drizzled with oil, grilled, and sprinkled with flaked salt. Slice leftovers and put in wraps for lunch.

⅓ cup (80 ml) balsamic vinegar

4 teaspoons (20 g) Dijon mustard

2 tablespoons (40 g) honey

2 teaspoons (10 ml) lemon juice

¼ teaspoon dried thyme

¼ teaspoon salt, divided

¼ teaspoon freshly ground black pepper, divided

2 tablespoons (28 ml) expeller-pressed grapeseed or canola oil, divided

1 pound (455 g) chicken breasts, pounded to ½-inch (1.3 cm) thickness, cut into 8 pieces

1 small yellow bell pepper, quartered lengthwise

1 small red bell pepper, quartered lengthwise

1 small green bell pepper, quartered lengthwise

1 small red onion, quartered through core end

2 teaspoons (9 g) cold butter, cubed

Whisk vinegar, mustard, honey, lemon, thyme, and ⅛ teaspoon each salt and pepper in a medium nonmetal bowl. Slowly drizzle in 1 tablespoon (15 ml) of oil while whisking. Pour half of the marinade into a small bowl and reserve. Add chicken to medium bowl of marinade and coat evenly. Chill the chicken and reserved marinade at least 30 minutes, up to overnight.

Preheat grill on medium heat, or 350°F (180°C, or gas mark 4). Toss peppers and onion with remaining tablespoon (15 ml) of oil, along with remaining salt and pepper. Remove chicken from the marinade. Oil the grill and place vegetables and chicken on grate. Cook vegetables until tender and chicken until done, about 5 minutes per side. Remove food from grill and cut vegetables into bite-size pieces.

Microwave the reserved fresh marinade for 30 seconds until hot. Whisk in the butter. Drizzle the sauce over the chicken and vegetables and serve warm.

 GO CLEAN

Canola oil has a high smoke point, making it an excellent choice for high-heat sautés, frying, and grilling. Its high proportion of heart-healthy omega-3 ALAs (alpha-linoleic acids) makes it a more nutritious choice than vegetable oil.

TOTAL PREP AND COOK TIME: 45 MINUTES, PLUS MARINATING TIME • YIELD: 4 SERVINGS, 2 PIECES CHICKEN EACH (WITH ½ CUP [75 G] VEGETABLES AND 1 TEASPOON (5 ML) SAUCE)

PER SERVING: 247 CALORIES; 10 G TOTAL FAT; 2 G SATURATED FAT; 30 G PROTEIN; 11 G CARBOHYDRATE; 1 G DIETARY FIBER; 71 MG CHOLESTEROL.

CHICKEN TORTILLA STEW WITH BLACK BEANS & GREEN CHILE

I lightened this recipe by baking, instead of deep-frying, the oil-spritzed tortilla chips. The added vegetables make this a hearty meal in one bowl.

1 pound (455 g) boneless skinless chicken thighs, cut into 1-inch (2.5 cm) pieces

1 (15-ounce, or 425 g) can black beans, rinsed and drained

1 (15-ounce, or 425 g) can diced tomatoes with juice

1 cup (160 g) sliced red onion

1 large green chile pepper, such as Anaheim, diced ¼ inch (6 mm)

2 teaspoons (6 g) minced garlic

3 tablespoons (48 g) tomato paste

½ cup (120 ml) organic or reduced sodium chicken broth

2½ teaspoons (6 g) ground cumin, divided

1½ teaspoons (4 g) chili powder

½ teaspoon salt, divided

½ teaspoon freshly ground black pepper

5 corn tortillas, stacked and cut into ¼-inch (6 mm) thick strips

Expeller-pressed canola oil spray

1 avocado, diced

¼ cup (60 g) nonfat plain Greek yogurt

To a slow cooker, add chicken, beans, tomatoes with juice, onions, chile peppers, garlic, tomato paste, broth, 2 teaspoons (5 g) cumin, chili powder, ¼ teaspoon salt, and pepper. Cover and cook on low for 5½ hours.

Meanwhile, preheat oven to 400°F (200°C, or gas mark 6). Spread tortillas on a large sheet pan and spray with oil. Sprinkle with remaining ½ teaspoon of cumin and ¼ teaspoon of salt, toss, and spread into an even layer. Bake for 16 minutes until golden, flipping halfway through. Arrange tortillas in serving bowls and ladle in the stew, placing the avocados, and adding a dollop of yogurt on top.

 GO GREEN

Anaheim chile peppers peak in mid-summer. If domestic fresh green chiles aren't available or you don't have one on hand, feel free to substitute green bell peppers or 2 (4.5-ounce, or 125 g) cans of green chiles.

TOTAL PREP AND COOK TIME: 6 HOURS • YIELD: 5 SERVINGS, 1⅓ CUPS (APPROX. 293 G) EACH (WITH A SMALL HANDFUL OF TORTILLA STRIPS, ⅕ AVOCADO, AND 1 TABLESPOON [15 G] YOGURT)

PER SERVING: 483 CALORIES; 14 G TOTAL FAT; 3 SATURATED FAT; 27 G PROTEIN; 45 G CARBOHYDRATE; 9 G DIETARY FIBER; 58 MG CHOLESTEROL.

CHICKEN PICCATA WITH LIGHT LEMON CAPER SAUCE

This is a favorite in my house on the weekends and for entertaining guests. I prepared this recipe for my crazy-busy mom friend and television show host Stephanie Sandoval after she had her baby. Now it's her go-to dish to prepare and deliver to friends and family. Serve with whole-grain pasta tossed with tomatoes and olive oil or rice pilaf.

1¼ pounds (570 g) chicken breast (about 3) or chicken breast fillets
¼ teaspoon salt
¼ teaspoon + 1 pinch freshly ground black pepper, divided
2 tablespoons (28 ml) extra-virgin olive oil
¼ cup (30 g) whole-wheat flour
2 tablespoons (28 ml) dry white wine
1 cup (235 ml) organic or reduced sodium chicken broth, divided
1 teaspoon (3 g) cornstarch
½ lemon (use center), peeled and cut into 4 thin slices, seeded
2 tablespoons (8 g) chopped Italian flat-leaf parsley
1 tablespoon (9 g) capers, chopped
1 tablespoon (14 g) butter

GO CLEAN

Organic and reduced sodium chicken broths rely more on chicken and vegetables for flavor rather than added salt.

Cut the chicken breasts to make 8 pieces total. Place chicken in a single layer on a cutting board and lay a sheet of plastic wrap on top. Pound the chicken with a mallet until pieces are an even ¼-inch (6 mm) thick. Season with salt and ¼ teaspoon pepper.

Heat a large skillet over medium heat and add oil. Pour flour onto a plate, coat chicken with flour, and shake pieces lightly to remove excess flour. When oil is shimmering, add chicken in a single layer, pressing down the center of each piece. After 1 minute, shake the pan gently back and forth to ensure even browning. Cook the chicken for 2 minutes or until it is opaque halfway through. Turn the chicken and continue to cook another 2 minutes or until cooked through. Remove the chicken from the pan and place it on a plate.

Add the wine to the pan, scraping browned bits from the bottom of the pan with a wooden spoon. Once the wine has evaporated to about 2 teaspoons (10 ml), add ¾ cup (175 ml) of broth and simmer for 5 minutes or until reduced by one-third. Whisk remaining ¼ cup (60 ml) of broth and cornstarch together in a small dish, add mixture to the pan, and bring to a simmer while stirring. Reduce heat to low and stir in lemons, parsley, capers, and a pinch of pepper. Smash the lemons lightly while cooking to release juices. Add the chicken back to the pan to reheat and coat with sauce. Turn the heat off and swirl in the butter.

 TOTAL PREP AND COOK TIME: 30 MINUTES • YIELD: 4 SERVINGS, 2 PIECES CHICKEN EACH (WITH 2 TABLESPOONS [28 ML] SAUCE)

PER SERVING: 281 CALORIES; 11 G TOTAL FAT; 3 G SATURATED FAT; 34 G PROTEIN; 7 G CARBOHYDRATE; 1 G DIETARY FIBER; 90 MG CHOLESTEROL.

ON-THE-GO TANGY CHICKEN, BELL PEPPER & RED POTATO PACKETS

The keys to success with this recipe are cutting the food into small enough pieces and level layering to ensure even cooking. You can package these ahead of time for cookouts or camping excursions, and for this purpose, I recommend using heavy-duty foil.

FOR PACKETS:

Expeller-pressed canola oil spray

8 small red potatoes, sliced ⅛-inch
(3 mm) thick (about 3¼ cups,
or 358 g)

1½ teaspoons (7.5 ml) extra-virgin olive oil

¼ teaspoon + 1 pinch salt, divided

¼ teaspoon + 1 pinch freshly ground
black pepper, divided

1 pound (455 g) chicken breast, cut into
¾-inch (2 cm) pieces

2 teaspoons (6 g) minced garlic

¼ teaspoon dried oregano

¼ teaspoon dried rosemary, crumbled
between fingers or chopped

1 red bell pepper, sliced into 8 to 12 thin
rings

4 teaspoons (20 g) cold butter

FOR VINAIGRETTE:

2 teaspoons (10 ml) balsamic vinegar

½ teaspoon Dijon mustard

½ teaspoon reduced sodium soy sauce

½ teaspoon honey

 GO GREEN

Red potatoes peak in late summer through early fall.

Preheat grill on medium-low, 325°F to 350°F (170°C to 180°C, or gas mark 3 to 4).

TO MAKE THE PACKETS: Tear aluminum foil into four 12 x 10-inch (30 x 25 cm) sheets or 12 x 12-inch (30 x 30 cm) sheets if you will be transporting the packets. Lightly coat foil with canola oil spray. Divide potatoes among pieces of foil, drizzle olive oil over potatoes, and sprinkle on ¼ teaspoon each of salt and pepper. Toss lightly to coat; spread potatoes in a single layer in the center of each piece of foil in an oval shape arranged lengthwise on each piece.

Toss the chicken in a medium bowl with garlic, oregano, and rosemary, and a pinch each of salt and pepper and spoon evenly over the potatoes. Top each potato with 2 to 3 pepper slices. Slice the butter into thin pieces and distribute evenly over the chicken.

Fold up the foil on all sides, allowing a 2 x 3-inch (5 x 7.5 cm) opening. If you will be transporting these, you may seal the pouches completely, but be sure to reopen them before grilling.

Place the pouches on the hottest part of the grill, close the grill lid, and cook for 25 minutes or until chicken is cooked through and potatoes are fork-tender.

TO MAKE THE VINAIGRETTE: Whisk together the vinaigrette ingredients in a small bowl. Remove the pouches from the grill and drizzle each with 1 teaspoon (5 ml) of the vinaigrette. Enjoy while hot, directly from the pouch.

TOTAL PREP AND COOK TIME: 1 HOUR • YIELD: 4 SERVINGS, 1 POUCH EACH

PER SERVING: 284 CALORIES; 7 G TOTAL FAT; 3 G SATURATED FAT; 29 G PROTEIN; 25 G CARBOHYDRATE; 3 G DIETARY FIBER; 76 MG CHOLESTEROL.

TURKEY, VEGETABLE & OAT MINI-MEATLOAVES WITH MARINARA SAUCE

I love that meatloaf can be mixed ahead of time and popped into the oven right before dinner, and making smaller loaves cuts cooking time by half. If you want to make the mixture ahead of time and refrigerate, just be sure to let it temper for 20 minutes on the counter before putting it in the oven to ensure more even cooking.

Expeller-pressed canola oil spray

1 (8-ounce, or 225 g) package crimini (baby bella) mushrooms (about 2½ cups)

1 small yellow onion, cut into eighths (1 cup, or 160 g)

4 cloves garlic (or 2 teaspoons [6 g] minced)

1 tablespoon (15 ml) extra-virgin olive oil

1 cup (80 g) dry rolled oats

2 large eggs

1 pound (455 g) lean ground turkey (or beef or bison)

1¾ cups (438 g) pasta sauce, divided

3 tablespoons (45 ml) red wine vinegar

1 tablespoon (6 g) Italian herb seasoning

½ teaspoon salt

½ teaspoon freshly ground black pepper

Preheat oven to 375°F (190°°C, or gas mark 5). Coat a 9 x 13-inch (23 x 33 cm) baking pan or six mini loaf pans with spray. Pulse mushrooms in a food processor until finely chopped and add them to a large bowl. Repeat with onion and garlic.

Place a large frying pan over medium heat and add oil. When oil is shimmering, add vegetables and sauté for 7 minutes or until water releases and evaporates completely, lowering the heat as necessary. Set aside.

Process the oats until they are of a fine consistency. Whisk the eggs in the bowl used for the vegetables. Add processed oats, turkey, ¾ cup (188 g) of pasta sauce, cooked vegetables, vinegar, Italian seasoning, salt, and pepper and stir together with a fork until blended.

Scoop the mixture into 6 mounds on the pan or into each mini-loaf pan, about ¾ cup (187 g) each. Shape each mound into a 4 x 2-inch (10 x 5 cm) loaf. Spread remaining 1 cup (250 g) of pasta sauce on top of the loaves, distributing evenly. Bake on middle rack for 25 minutes, turning pan midway through cooking, until loaves are firm or a thermometer inserted in the middle reads at least 165°F (74°C). Allow loaves to rest for 5 minutes before serving.

 GO GREEN

Good-tasting pasta sauces don't have to come all the way from Italy. Opt for one made with domestically grown tomatoes. Just read the label.

 RECIPE NOTES

» You can finely chop vegetables with a knife rather than using a food processor if you prefer.

» Whole oats can be added to the meat mixture for a more rustic texture.

TOTAL PREP AND COOK TIME: 55 MINUTES • YIELD: 6 SERVINGS, 1 LOAF EACH

PER SERVING: 330 CALORIES; 12 G TOTAL FAT; 3 G SATURATED FAT; 23 G PROTEIN; 32 G CARBOHYDRATE; 5 G DIETARY FIBER; 115 MG CHOLESTEROL.

QUICK-BROILED OPEN-FACED TURKEY SWISS SANDWICHES WITH SPINACH & AVOCADO

I will go just about anywhere for a good meal. A couple of summers ago, my husband Steve and I braved it to Paris, with then fifteen-month-old Scarlet. One of our favorite dishes was croque-monsieur, a classic French sandwich made with ham, Gruyere cheese, and béchamel sauce broiled to perfection. I add my personal touch in this version using natural turkey and, of course, a handful of vegetables that turns the recipe into a complete meal. Recipe tester Melissa liked that it is so easy to make for lunch and is looking forward to trying it with leftover dinner meats. Her kids just loved eating it, too!

4 large slices whole-wheat bread
2 tablespoons (28 ml) olive oil mayonnaise
2 teaspoons (10 g) Dijon mustard
4 cups (120 g) baby spinach, chopped once through
8 (0.75-ounce, or 21 g) slices natural roasted turkey (reduced sodium preferred)
4 (1-ounce, or 28 g) slices Swiss cheese (such as a sharp Gruyere or Emmenthal), cut in half
1 avocado, sliced thin
1 large tomato, sliced thin
Freshly ground black pepper

Place oven rack on second highest shelf, about 3 inches (7.5 cm) under heating element, and preheat to a low broil. Place bread on a sheet pan in a single layer and broil for 1 to 2 minutes until toasted on top. Remove the pan from the oven.

Remove the bread from the pan and spread mayonnaise and mustard on untoasted side of each slice. Lay spinach, turkey, and cheese on top. Place the bread back on the pan and broil for 4 to 5 minutes until cheese bubbles and begins to brown. Remove from the oven. Arrange the avocado and tomato on top and sprinkle on the pepper. Serve warm with a fork and a knife. Cut into strips for little ones to pick up with their fingers.

 GO CLEAN

Convincing evidence indicates that processed meats (preserved by smoking, curing, salting, or added chemical preservatives) are a cause of colorectal cancer and should be avoided (World Cancer Research Fund and American Institute for Cancer Research Panel, 2007). Substitute nitrate-free and lower sodium versions whenever possible.

 TOTAL PREP AND COOK TIME: 15 MINUTES • YIELD: 4 SERVINGS, 1 SANDWICH EACH

PER SERVING: 323 CALORIES; 18 G TOTAL FAT; 6 G SATURATED FAT; 20 G PROTEIN; 20 G CARBOHYDRATE; 5 G DIETARY FIBER; 38 MG CHOLESTEROL.

HEARTY CUBAN CHICKEN WITH WHOLE-GRAIN TOMATO OLIVE RICE

An old friend of mine learned this dish from his Cuban grandmother, and then he passed it on to me. I bulked it up with more vegetables by adding corn, peppers, and peas. The briny olives balance the dish deliciously.

1 tablespoon (15 ml) expeller-pressed grapeseed or canola oil, divided

1½ pounds (680 g) chicken breast (cut into 6 pieces)

½ teaspoon salt, divided

½ teaspoon freshly ground black pepper, divided

1 small onion, diced ¼ inch, or 6 mm (1 cup, or 160 g)

1 medium green bell pepper, diced ¼ inch or 6 mm (about ¾ cup, or 112 g)

2 teaspoons (6 g) minced garlic

1 (15-ounce, 425 g) can diced tomatoes in juice

1½ cups (355 ml) organic or reduced sodium chicken broth

¼ cup (25 g) sliced green olives with pimientos with 3 tablespoons (45 ml) olive brine

1 teaspoon (3 g) chili powder

½ teaspoon ground cumin

1 cup (185 g) brown rice, raw

1 cup (164 g) corn kernels, fresh or frozen, thawed

1 cup (130 g) frozen peas, thawed

¼ cup (4 g) chopped cilantro

1½ teaspoons (7.5 ml) lime juice

Heat a large skillet over medium-high heat and add 2 teaspoons (10 ml) of the canola oil. Season the chicken with ¼ teaspoon each of salt and pepper. When oil is shimmering, add the chicken, rounded side down, and cook for 3 minutes until browned on one side. Move the chicken to a plate and lower the heat to medium.

Pour 1 teaspoon (5 ml) of canola oil into the pan and add onion, bell pepper, and garlic. Cook until translucent on medium-low heat, about 3 minutes, scraping up brown bits with a wooden spoon and lowering heat as necessary. Add tomatoes, broth, olives, chili powder, and cumin, along with remaining ¼ teaspoon each salt and pepper, and bring to a boil on high heat. Stir in rice and bring to a boil. Reduce heat to low, cover, and simmer for 30 minutes. Add chicken, corn, and peas. Cover and simmer for 20 minutes, until rice becomes tender and absorbs most of the liquid. The rice should be somewhat loose, not completely stiff. Stir in cilantro and lime juice and serve hot.

 RECIPE NOTE

Use the remaining cilantro in pesto or rice, stir into soups, or toss small sprigs into green salads. The soft stems are edible, too. Cilantro does not last long, especially after washing.

TOTAL PREP AND COOK TIME: 50 MINUTES • YIELD: 6 SERVINGS, 1 PIECE CHICKEN EACH (WITH 1 CUP [195 G] RICE)

PER SERVING: 325 CALORIES; 6 G TOTAL FAT; 1 G SATURATED FAT; 31 G PROTEIN; 37 G CARBOHYDRATE; 4 G DIETARY FIBER; 66 MG CHOLESTEROL.

JAMAICAN JERK CHICKEN & SWEET POTATO PLANKS

On cold nights when I don't feel like using the grill, I just pop this meal into a 375°F (190°C or gas mark 5) oven for about 45 minutes.

FOR CHICKEN:

¼ small yellow onion
2 scallions, cut into thirds
1 jalapeño pepper, stemmed, halved, seeds and membrane removed
2 tablespoons (28 ml) fresh orange juice
2 tablespoons (28 ml) red wine vinegar
1 tablespoon (16 g) Jamaican jerk seasoning (buy or make your own*)
1 tablespoon (15 ml) expeller-pressed grapeseed or canola oil
1 tablespoon (15 g) packed brown sugar
1 tablespoon (15 g) Dijon mustard
1 garlic clove
1 teaspoon salt
3 bone-in, skin-on chicken breasts (about 2½ pounds, or 1.1 kg), halved
Expeller-pressed grapeseed or canola oil spray

FOR SWEET POTATOES:

3 medium sweet potatoes, sliced cross-wise into ¾-inch (2 cm)-thick circles
1 tablespoon (15 ml) expeller-pressed grapeseed or canola oil
⅛ teaspoon salt
⅛ teaspoon freshly ground black pepper

TO MAKE THE CHICKEN: Put all the ingredients except the chicken into a food processor and run until puréed to create a marinade. Place chicken and marinade in a shallow dish. Spoon the marinade over and under the skin and refrigerate for at least 1 hour, up to overnight.

Preheat the grill on medium low (about 325°F, 170°C or gas mark 3).

TO MAKE THE SWEET POTATOES: Coat the potatoes in oil, salt, and pepper.

Coat a sheet of aluminum foil with oil spray, place on the hottest part of the grill and lay the chicken skin side down on the foil. Put the potatoes directly on the grate, over the cooler side of the grill or in a grill basket. Cook for 10 minutes. Rotate the chicken by one-quarter and turn the potatoes. Cook for an additional 10 minutes. Remove potatoes from grill when fork-tender. Turn chicken and cook for 15 to 20 minutes until juices run clear or an instant-read thermometer inserted into the middle reaches 165°F (74°C). Allow chicken to rest for 5 minutes before serving.

 RECIPE NOTE

*Make your own Jamaican jerk seasoning by combining ½ teaspoon each dried thyme leaves (or 2 tablespoons [5 g] fresh), dried rosemary leaves (or 1 tablespoon [2 g] fresh), freshly ground black pepper, and ginger powder; ¼ teaspoon each ground cloves, ground nutmeg, ground allspice; and ⅛ teaspoon ground cinnamon.

TOTAL PREP AND COOK TIME: 55 MINUTES, PLUS MARINATING TIME • YIELD: 6 SERVINGS, ½ CHICKEN BREAST EACH (WITH ½ CUP [113 G] SWEET POTATOES)

PER SERVING: 330 CALORIES; 7 G TOTAL FAT; 1 G SATURATED FAT; 45 G PROTEIN; 19 G CARBOHYDRATE; 2 G DIETARY FIBER; 110 MG CHOLESTEROL.

 GO GREEN

Jalapeño peppers peak in summer and early fall. Substitute with 1 teaspoon (2 g) dried jalapeño when domestically grown peppers are unavailable.

TURKEY VEGETABLE POT PIE WITH WHOLE-WHEAT CRUST

Don't let homemade pie crust intimidate you, especially this one, which is so forgiving. I rationalized that if apples can go into a pie raw and come out tender, so can turkey and vegetables. The result? Streamlined and tantalizing!

FOR CRUST:

1 cup (120 g) whole-wheat flour
1 cup (125 g) all-purpose flour
¼ teaspoon salt
⅔ cup (160 ml) corn oil
⅓ cup (80 ml) orange juice

FOR FILLING:

1 (10- to 12-ounce [280 to 340 g]) carton condensed cream of chicken soup (organic preferred)
½ cup (120 ml) low-fat milk
1¼ pound (570 g) boneless, skinless turkey breast, thinly sliced into bite-size pieces
1 cup (130 g) thinly sliced carrots (or frozen sliced carrots, thawed)
1 cup (89 g) leeks, quartered lengthwise, then thinly sliced crosswise, using white and pale green parts only
¾ cup (65 g) thinly sliced celery
½ cup (75 g) frozen peas, thawed
3 tablespoons (23 g) whole-wheat flour
2 teaspoons (2 g) dried herbes de Provence (or ½ teaspoon each thyme, rosemary, and basil)
2 teaspoons (4 g) grated lemon zest
½ teaspoon freshly ground black pepper
¼ teaspoon salt

TO MAKE THE CRUST: Combine flours and salt in a medium bowl. Pour in oil and orange juice and stir until moistened. Press dough to flatten and chill.

TO MAKE THE FILLING: Blend soup and ½ cup (120 ml) of milk in a large bowl. Mix in the remaining ingredients.

Preheat oven to 350°F (180°C, or gas mark 4). Divide dough into 2 balls, one slightly larger than the other. Roll the larger ball between 2 large sheets of waxed paper until it is ⅛-inch (3 mm)-thick or until it fits in the bottom of a 9-inch (23 cm) pie pan. Remove the top sheet of waxed paper. Turn dough over and carefully place in the pie pan, removing remaining piece of waxed paper. Press out any bubbles and patch holes with scraps of dough. Pour filling into the prepared pan. Roll remaining dough and lay it on top. Cut any excess dough hanging from the edges and crimp the crust between your thumb and forefinger to seal. Cut a heart into the center to allow steam to escape.

Place the pie on a sheet pan and bake for 1 hour and 15 minutes, until center of crust becomes golden and an instant-read thermometer inserted into the pie's center reaches 165°F (74°C), covering browned edges only with foil about halfway through cooking. Remove the pie from the oven and allow it to rest for at least 5 minutes before cutting.

TOTAL PREP AND COOK TIME: 2 HOURS 15 MINUTES • YIELD: 6 SERVINGS, 1 PIECE EACH

PER SERVING: 542 CALORIES; 30 G TOTAL FAT; 5 G SATURATED FAT; 22 G PROTEIN; 47 G CARBOHYDRATE; 5 G DIETARY FIBER; 77 MG CHOLESTEROL.

 RECIPE NOTE

You can substitute 3¾ cups (525 g) cooked, diced chicken for the turkey.

HOISIN CHICKEN & BOK CHOY STIR-FRY

Hoisin sauce, found in the Asian food section, is the Chinese version of BBQ sauce and instantly adds depth to recipes.

2 tablespoons (28 ml) expeller-pressed grapeseed or canola oil, divided

1 pound (455 g) chicken breast, thinly sliced against the grain into bite-size strips

1 (8-ounce, or 225 g) package cremini (baby bella) mushrooms, quartered (about 2½ cups)

1 tablespoon (10 g) minced garlic

1 tablespoon (6 g) minced ginger (or ¾ teaspoon ginger powder)

6 cups (420 g) ½-inch (1.3 cm)-thick sliced bok choy

3 tablespoons (45 ml) reduced sodium soy sauce

2 tablespoons (31 g) Hoisin sauce (or sweet barbecue sauce)

1 tablespoon (15 ml) rice vinegar

2 teaspoons (5 g) cornstarch

1 teaspoon (7 g) honey

¼ teaspoon freshly ground black pepper

2 tablespoons (16 g) toasted sesame seeds (if using raw, cook with the garlic and ginger)

3 cups (585 g) hot cooked brown rice

Heat a large sauté pan or wok over medium-high heat and add 1 tablespoon (15 ml) of oil. When oil is shimmering, add chicken and cook undisturbed for 2 minutes; then stir-fry for 2 minutes. Remove chicken from the pan. Add remaining tablespoon (15 ml) of oil to the pan over medium heat and stir in mushrooms. Cook for 3 minutes until the liquid releases and the mushrooms brown. Add garlic and ginger* and cook for 30 seconds until fragrant. Add bok choy and cook for 3 minutes.

In a small bowl, blend soy sauce, Hoisin sauce, vinegar, cornstarch, honey, and pepper. Add the cooked chicken and sauce to the vegetables and cook over medium-high for 2 minutes, until the sauce thickens. Sprinkle with sesame seeds and serve with rice.

GO GREEN

Bok choy peaks in late fall through early spring. You can substitute with 3 cups (340 g) of 3 x ¼-inch (7.5 cm x 6 mm) strips of summer squash during summer months.

RECIPE NOTE

You can substitute tofu for the chicken. Rinse 1 (16-ounce, or 455 g) block of extra-firm tofu under water and wrap in 3 layers of a paper towel. Put the tofu on a plate, place another heavy plate on top of the tofu to weigh it down, and chill for 30 minutes, up to overnight. Unwrap the tofu and cut it into pinky-finger-size strips by slicing crosswise into 7 pieces, and then cutting each slice into quarters. Blot with a towel. Heat a large frying pan or wok over medium-high heat and add 1 tablespoon (15 ml) of canola oil. When the oil begins to shimmer, add the tofu in a single layer. Brown the tofu, without stirring, for 3 to 4 minutes. Turn the pieces over, cook for 2 more minutes, and remove from the pan. Continue with the recipe.

TOTAL PREP AND COOK TIME: 45 MINUTES • YIELD: 5 SERVINGS, 1¼ CUPS (APPROX. 225 G) STIR-FRY EACH (WITH ¾ CUP [146 G] RICE)

PER SERVING: 337 CALORIES; 9 G TOTAL FAT; 1 G SATURATED FAT; 27 G PROTEIN; 36 G CARBOHYDRATE; 4 G DIETARY FIBER; 53 MG CHOLESTEROL.

SIZZLING SESAME NOODLES WITH PORK, CABBAGE & SCALLIONS

Pork lo mein is one of our all-time favorite Chinese takeout dishes. I cleaned up the traditional recipe and added vegetables to my home-cooked version. This recipe provides plenty of leftovers and tastes even better the next day.

FOR STIR-FRY:

1¼ pounds (570 g) pork tenderloin or sirloin, cut into 1½ x ¼-inch (38 x 6 mm) strips

1 tablespoon (15 ml) reduced sodium soy sauce

1 (10-ounce, or 280 g) package Japanese udon, Chinese lo mein, or fettuccine noodles

2 tablespoons (28 ml) expeller-pressed grapeseed or canola oil

3 cups (210 g) shredded green cabbage

1 red bell pepper, cut into thin strips (about 2 cups, or 300 g)

4 scallions, sliced crosswise into 1½-inch (3.8 cm) pieces, then thinly sliced lengthwise (½ cup, or 50 g)

1 tablespoon (10 g) minced garlic

1 tablespoon (6 g) minced ginger

1 teaspoon (5 ml) reduced sodium soy sauce

1 tablespoon (8 g) toasted sesame seeds

FOR SAUCE:

3 tablespoons (45 ml) rice vinegar (or white distilled vinegar)

4 teaspoons (20 ml) reduced sodium soy sauce

1 tablespoon (20 g) chile or (15 g) garlic black bean sauce

2 teaspoons (10 ml) dark sesame oil

1 teaspoon (7 g) honey

1 teaspoon (2 g) Chinese 5-spice powder (or ¼ teaspoon cinnamon and ⅛ teaspoon each ground fennel and cloves)

1 teaspoon (5 ml) rice wine, dry sherry, or vermouth

⅛ teaspoon freshly ground white pepper (or ¼ teaspoon freshly ground black pepper)

Marinate the pork in the soy sauce for 20 minutes.

TO MAKE THE STIR-FRY: Cook according to package directions in a large pot until al dente. Rinse with cold water and then drain.

TO MAKE THE SAUCE: In a separate bowl, stir all the sauce ingredients together.

Heat the noodle pot or a large wok over medium heat and add 1 tablespoon (15 ml) of the oil. When oil is shimmering, add cabbage, bell pepper, scallions, garlic, ginger, and soy sauce and stir-fry for 5 minutes until tender. Push vegetables to one side; add remaining tablespoon (15 ml) of oil and pork to the pan, arranging pork in a single layer. Cook undisturbed for 2 minutes to brown and then stir-fry until cooked through. Add noodles and sesame seeds and stir-fry for 1 minute. Stir in the sauce and cook for 1 minute.

 GO GREEN

Cabbage is a cool-season crop, peaking in spring and fall.

TOTAL PREP AND COOK TIME: 45 MINUTES • YIELD: 5 SERVINGS, 1½ CUPS (APPROX. 287 G) EACH

PER SERVING: 424 CALORIES; 12 G TOTAL FAT; 2 G SATURATED FAT; 29 G PROTEIN; 51 G CARBOHYDRATE; 4 G DIETARY FIBER; 56 MG CHOLESTEROL.

ORANGE PEEL BEEF & BROCCOLI STIR-FRY WITH BROWN RICE

I concocted this meal when I was a private chef and it instantly became a client favorite. It boasts a flavor profile that appeals to kids and adults, very easy preparation, and quick clean-up.

FOR SAUCE:

2 tablespoons (28 ml) reduced sodium soy sauce

1 tablespoon + 2 teaspoons (25 ml) rice vinegar

1 tablespoon (8 g) cornstarch

2 teaspoons (14 g) honey

½ teaspoon freshly ground black pepper

¼ teaspoon Chinese 5-spice powder (or ¼ teaspoon cinnamon and ⅛ teaspoon each ground fennel and cloves)

1 tablespoon (15 ml) dark sesame oil

FOR STIR-FRY:

5½ cups (390 g) bite-size broccoli florets

1 tablespoon (10 g) minced garlic

1 tablespoon (6 g) minced ginger (or ½ teaspoon ground ginger)

⅛ teaspoon salt

1 pound (455 g) flank or flat iron steak, or top sirloin, thinly sliced against the grain in 1½-inch (3.8 cm) pieces

1 tablespoon (15 ml) expeller-pressed grapeseed or canola oil

1 orange, 2 teaspoons (4 g) grated zest, inner segments sliced

2 teaspoons (5 g) sesame seeds

3 cups (585 g) cooked brown rice

TO MAKE THE SAUCE: Stir together all of the sauce ingredients in a small bowl and set aside.

TO MAKE THE STIR-FRY: Heat a large frying pan or wok over high heat, add 1 cup (235 ml) of water, and bring to a boil. Add broccoli, reduce heat to a low boil, and cover with a lid or piece of foil, leaving a gap for steam to escape. Steam for 5 minutes until almost fork-tender. Move broccoli to a plate, reserving cooking water in another container.

In a medium bowl, sprinkle garlic, ginger, and salt evenly over the beef. Scrape the pan clean, place it on high heat, and add the oil. When oil is shimmering, add the beef in an even layer and cook for 2 minutes undisturbed until brown. Toss with a wooden spoon to break up the pieces, reducing heat to medium-high as needed. Add orange zest and sesame seeds and cook until beef is done, another 2 minutes. Swirl in the sauce, add broccoli, and stir-fry to reheat. Add a splash of reserved broccoli water if mixture seems too dry. Serve hot and garnish with orange segments.

 GO CLEAN

Replace Japanese soy sauce with a domestic soy sauce, which is still authentically manufactured but doesn't require a gas-guzzling trip overseas.

TOTAL PREP AND COOKING TIME: 45 MINUTES • YIELD: 4 SERVINGS, 1 CUP (APPROX. 215 G) STIR-FRY EACH (WITH ¾ CUP [146 G] RICE)

PER SERVING: 476 CALORIES; 15 G TOTAL FAT; 3 G SATURATED FAT; 32 G PROTEIN; 55 G CARBOHYDRATE; 10 G DIETARY FIBER; 71 MG CHOLESTEROL.

SLOW COOKER BEEF & VEGETABLE TACOS

Taco night reigns as a family favorite in countless households, along with the ubiquitous taco seasoning packet. This recipe delivers the same sultry flavor, without all the additives in the mystery pouch. Simmering the ingredients in a slow cooker allows the vegetables to virtually melt into the meat, hidden from the pickiest eaters.

1 (3.4-ounce, or 95 g) package shiitake
   mushrooms, stems removed
   (or 1 [8-ounce, or 225 g] package
   cremini mushrooms)
1 small onion, quartered (about 1 cup,
   or 160 g)
3 cloves garlic
1 celery stalk, cut into chunks
1 pound (455 g) organic ground beef
   or bison
½ cup (120 ml) organic beef broth
1 (6-ounce, or 170 g) can tomato paste
1 tablespoon (15 ml) lime juice
1 tablespoon (15 ml) reduced sodium soy
   sauce
2 teaspoons (5 g) chili powder
2 teaspoons (5 g) paprika
2 teaspoons (5 g) ground cumin
¼ teaspoon dried oregano
¼ teaspoon salt
¼ teaspoon freshly ground black pepper
8 small or 4 large whole-grain flour tortillas, warmed
Toppings: sliced avocado, nonfat plain
   Greek yogurt, salsa, shredded cheese,
   and diced tomatoes

Separately whir mushrooms, onion, garlic, and celery in a food processor until finely chopped. In a slow cooker, mix together beef, chopped vegetables, broth, tomato paste, lime juice, soy sauce, chili powder, paprika, cumin, oregano, salt, and pepper. Cover and cook on low for 5 hours until vegetables become extremely tender and practically melt into the meat. Stir thoroughly, breaking up any remaining chunks of meat.

Serve with tortillas and toppings.

 GO GREEN

Shiitake mushrooms, available year-round, develop a meaty, almost woodsy flavor when cooked, bulking up meat dishes and adding ergothioneine (an antioxidant), riboflavin, niacin, pantothenic acid, and copper.

 RECIPE NOTES

I find that the most efficient way to wash mushrooms is to give them a quick dunk in water, brushing off peat moss with fingers. Lift them out of the water and drain thoroughly. Never soak mushrooms, since they easily absorb moisture.

TOTAL PREP AND COOK TIME: 5½ HOURS • YIELD: 6 SERVINGS, 2 TACOS OR 1 BURRITO EACH

PER SERVING: 394 CALORIES; 12 G TOTAL FAT; 4 G SATURATED FAT; 24 G PROTEIN; 47 G CARBOHYDRATE; 6 G DIETARY FIBER; 47 MG CHOLESTEROL.

STEVE'S FAMOUS TAILGATE CHILI WITH KIDNEY BEANS

Because they require so much work, our big game-day parties have gone by the way-side since Scarlet was born. Even so, friends still rave about this chili. Now we're happy to enjoy it while relaxing and watching the game from home. A healthful condiment bar is served alongside to round out this heart-warming stew. Whole-grain corn muffins with corn kernels and green chiles also make a delicious complement. This recipe is very easy to prepare, and it cooks for 6 hours in the slow cooker, freeing you up for pregame fun.

2 teaspoons (10 ml) expeller-pressed grapeseed or canola oil

1 pound (455 g) bottom or eye-of-round beef, cubed ¼ inch (6 mm)

½ teaspoon salt

½ teaspoon freshly ground black pepper

2 tablespoons (15 g) chili powder

½ teaspoon ground cumin

½ teaspoon paprika

1 small yellow onion, sliced (1½ cups, or 240 g)

1 (14.5-ounce, or 410 g) can crushed tomatoes

1 (14.5-ounce, or 410 g) can red kidney beans, rinsed and drained

¼ cup (60 ml) organic beef broth

3 garlic cloves, minced

1 teaspoon (5 ml) lime juice

¼ teaspoon dried oregano

Toppings: chopped tomatoes, sliced scallions, diced avocado, and nonfat plain Greek yogurt

Heat a large skillet over high heat. Add the oil and once it begins to shimmer, add the beef, salt, and pepper, and brown for 4 minutes, reducing the heat if needed. Sprinkle in chili powder, cumin, and paprika to toast during the last 20 seconds. Add 2 tablespoons (28 ml) of water and scrape up any brown bits with a wooden spoon. Add beef and remaining ingredients (except toppings) to the slow cooker. Cover and cook on low for 5 to 6 hours until onions and beef are tender. Serve hot with toppings. Can be stored chilled for up to 4 days.

 GO CLEAN

» Rinsing canned beans reduces sodium by 41 percent and removes much of the beans' hard-to-digest natural sugars.

» Tempeh, a cake of fermented soybeans, offers a nutty taste and hearty texture and may be used in place of beef for a lower carbon footprint. Crumble the tempeh with your hands and cook it over medium heat in oil. You can find tempeh in the refrigerated section of natural food stores.

TOTAL PREP AND COOK TIME: 6 HOURS • YIELD: 4 SERVINGS, 1 ROUNDED CUP (APPROX. 369 G) EACH

PER SERVING: 271 CALORIES; 7 G TOTAL FAT; 2 G SATURATED FAT; 29 G PROTEIN; 17 G CARBOHYDRATE; 6 G DIETARY FIBER; 53 MG CHOLESTEROL.

BRAISED PORK BUNS WITH QUICK PICKLED CUCUMBERS & BEAN SPROUTS

An extremely picky teen eater rated this dish a 20 on a scale from 1 to 10! The cabbage and onions become so tender that they blend in, disguised as meat.

FOR PORK:

2 teaspoons (10 ml) expeller-pressed grapeseed or canola oil

3.15 pounds (1.4 kg) Boston butt, cut into 3 pieces along natural muscle separation, trimmed of surface fat

½ teaspoon salt

½ teaspoon freshly ground black pepper

¼ cup (60 ml) vermouth, rice wine, or dry sherry

2½ cups (175 g) thinly sliced red cabbage

1 small onion, sliced (about 1 cup, or 160 g)

3 tablespoons (60 g) molasses (or honey)

2 tablespoons (28 ml) reduced sodium soy sauce

2 tablespoons (20 g) minced garlic

2 tablespoons (12 g) minced ginger

1 tablespoon (8 g) toasted sesame seeds

FOR CUCUMBERS:

1 tablespoon (20 g) honey

⅛ teaspoon salt

3 tablespoons (42 ml) rice vinegar

2 large cucumbers, peeled, cut in half lengthwise, seeded with a spoon, thinly sliced

⅛ teaspoon freshly ground black pepper

TO ASSEMBLE:

11 soft whole-wheat hamburger buns

2¾ cups (286 g) mungbean sprouts

TO MAKE THE PORK: Heat a large skillet over medium-high heat and add the oil. Season the pork on all sides with salt and pepper. When oil begins to shimmer, add pork and brown on all sides, about 4 minutes per side. Add browned pork to a slow cooker. Off of the heat, add the vermouth and then place on low heat, scraping up any brown bits from the bottom of the skillet with a wooden spoon. Add contents of the skillet to the slow cooker, along with cabbage, onion, molasses, soy sauce, garlic, ginger, and sesame seeds. Cover and cook on high for 1 hour; then reduce heat to low and cook for 4 hours*.

TO MAKE THE CUCUMBERS: One hour before serving, in a medium bowl, stir and dissolve the honey and salt into the rice vinegar and then add the cucumbers and pepper. Chill.

TO ASSEMBLE: Toast the buns cut side up under a broiler or in a toaster oven. Fill the buns with pork, drained cucumbers, and bean sprouts.

 RECIPE NOTES

» Boston butt is part of the shoulder. If you purchase the whole shoulder, ask your butcher to portion out 3.15 pounds (or 3 pounds [1.4 kg] after trimming).

» *Alternatively, cook the pork on low for the entire duration, 6 to 7 hours.

TOTAL PREP AND COOK TIME: 5½ HOURS • YIELD: 11 SERVINGS, 1 SANDWICH EACH (WITH ¼ CUP [30 G] CUCUMBERS AND ¼ CUP [26 G] SPROUTS

PER SERVING: 460 CALORIES; 18 G TOTAL FAT; 5 G SATURATED FAT; 31 G PROTEIN; 44 G CARBOHYDRATE; 7 G DIETARY FIBER; 76 MG CHOLESTEROL.

SLOW-SIMMERED BEEF VEGETABLE STEW WITH CANNELLINI BEANS

One of the best meals I ever ate was at the bottom of the Grand Canyon at Phantom Ranch while hiking this worldly wonder from rim to rim. I reinvented that hearty recipe here, lightening it with more vegetables and adding creamy cannellini beans. Serve with crusty whole-grain bread or dinner rolls.

1 tablespoon (15 ml) expeller-pressed grapeseed or canola oil

1 pound (455 g) beef stew meat, cut into large bite-size chunks

½ teaspoon freshly ground black pepper, divided

¼ teaspoon salt

¼ cup (60 ml) red wine

4 medium red potatoes, cut into bite-size chunks (about 2 cups, or 220 g)

1½ cups (240 g) white or red peeled pearl onions

2 carrots, cut into 1-inch (2.5 cm) chunks (about 1½ cups, or 195 g)

2 celery stalks, cut into 1-inch (2.5 cm) chunks (about ⅔ cup, or 67 g)

2 tablespoons (28 ml) red wine vinegar

2 natural beef bouillon cubes, crumbled

1 tablespoon (10 g) minced garlic (or 1½ teaspoons [4.5 g] garlic powder)

1 teaspoon dried herbes de Provence (or Italian herb seasoning)

⅛ teaspoon ground cloves

2 tablespoons (16 g) cornstarch

1 (15.5-ounce or 450 g) can cannellini beans, rinsed and drained

1 cup (100 g) green beans, cut into bite-size pieces

Heat a large skillet over high heat and add the oil. When oil begins to shimmer, sprinkle ¼ teaspoon of pepper, along with salt, onto the beef and add the beef to the skillet in a single layer; let the beef cook undisturbed for 2 minutes to brown. When it is browned on one side, stir the beef to brown it on all sides; do not cook it through. Add the beef to the slow cooker. Reduce heat to medium and move the skillet off of the burner. Pour the wine into the skillet and return the skillet to the burner, using a wooden spoon to scrape any brown bits from the bottom of the pan. Add the contents of the skillet to the slow cooker, along with the potatoes, onions, 1½ cups (355 ml) of water, carrots, celery, vinegar, bouillon, garlic, herbs, remaining ¼ teaspoon pepper, and cloves. Cover and simmer on low for 5 to 6 hours, until beef and vegetables are tender.

In a medium bowl, stir together the cornstarch and 2 tablespoons (28 ml) of water; add the cornstarch slurry and the cannellini and green beans to the slow cooker and stir well. Increase the heat to high for 30 minutes to thicken.

 RECIPE NOTES

» Peeled white pearl onions are available frozen and work well here. No need to thaw.

» If you can find packaged, rich demi-glace concentrate (in upscale markets), substitute ½ cup (120 ml) of reconstituted demi-glace for 1 bouillon cube and ½ cup (120 ml) of water.

TOTAL PREP AND COOK TIME: 6 TO 7 HOURS • YIELD: 6 SERVINGS, ABOUT 1½ CUPS (APPROX. 286 G) EACH

PER SERVING: 308 CALORIES; 11 G TOTAL FAT; 4 G SATURATED FAT; 20 G PROTEIN; 31 G CARBOHYDRATE; 5 G DIETARY FIBER; 43 MG CHOLESTEROL.

SUNDAY DINNER BOLOGNESE WITH WHOLE-WHEAT ZITI

I gleaned the gelatin trick from *Cook's Illustrated* to mimic a restaurant-quality stock even when you're just using boxed broth.

4 teaspoons (9 g) unflavored gelatin

1 cup (235 ml) organic beef broth

2 tablespoons (28 ml) extra-virgin olive oil

1 pound (455 g) ground organic or grass-fed lean beef or bison

2 (2-ounce, or 55 g) nitrate-free chicken or turkey sausage links, removed from casings

1 medium carrot, cut into large chunks

1 celery stalk, cut into large chunks

1 small yellow onion, quartered

3 garlic cloves

1 (6-ounce, or 170 g) can tomato paste

1 cup (235 ml) dry red wine

1 teaspoon dried sage

½ teaspoon salt

¼ teaspoon freshly ground black pepper

1 (14-ounce, or 390 g) box dry whole-grain ziti or penne pasta

¾ cup (75 g) grated Parmesan cheese

Sprinkle gelatin over broth, allowing it to dissolve on its own. Set aside. Heat a large skillet over high heat and pour in the oil. When oil begins to shimmer, add beef and sausage and break into smaller pieces with a wooden spoon to cover the entire bottom of the pan in a single layer. Cook meat undisturbed until it is browned on one side, about 4 minutes; then turn meat and break it into smaller pieces. Brown and cook for 4 minutes, reducing heat as liquid evaporates.

Meanwhile, whir the carrot chunks in a food processor until they are chopped into small bits and add them to the pan; repeat with celery and then with onion and garlic. Cook for 6 minutes over medium heat until tender. Stir in the tomato paste and cook until rust-colored and aromatic, about 5 minutes. Pour in the wine and simmer for 5 minutes until liquid has almost completely evaporated, scraping any brown bits from the bottom of the pan with a wooden spoon. Add broth, sage, salt, and pepper and simmer on medium-low heat until sauce becomes thick enough to leave a trail behind when you draw a spoon through it, about 30 minutes.

Meanwhile, boil the pasta in a large pot according to package directions. Drain, reserving ⅓ cup (80 ml) of the cooking water, and add pasta and reserved water back to the pot. Toss with sauce and serve hot with Parmesan cheese.

 GO CLEAN

Bison, commonly known as buffalo, is lower in total and saturated fats than other ground meats and has a much milder taste than you might think. Buffalos spend most of their lives grazing naturally and very little, if any, time on feedlots. Regulations prohibit the use of subtherapeutic antibiotics and artificial growth hormones in bison.

TOTAL PREP AND COOK TIME: 1 HOUR 10 MINUTES • YIELD: 8 SERVINGS, 1½ CUPS (126 G) EACH (WITH 1½ TABLESPOONS [7.5 G] PARMESAN)

PER SERVING: 409 CALORIES; 13 G TOTAL FAT; 4 G SATURATED FAT; 28 G PROTEIN; 41 G CARBOHYDRATE; 5 G DIETARY FIBER; 48 MG CHOLESTEROL.

GRILLED ROSEMARY DIJON PORK CHOP & VEGETABLE SKEWERS

This recipe offers a flavorful alternative to panfrying pork chops—and much less cleanup too!

- 3 tablespoons (45 ml) liquid amino acids (in natural food section, or reduced sodium soy sauce)
- 2 tablespoons (30 g) Dijon mustard
- 2 tablespoons (28 ml) apple cider vinegar
- 2 teaspoons (1.5 g) chopped rosemary (or ½ teaspoon dried, crumbled)
- 1 teaspoon (5 ml) reduced sodium Worcestershire sauce
- 1 teaspoon (2 g) freshly ground black pepper
- 1 tablespoon (10 g) minced garlic
- 2 tablespoons (28 ml) expeller-pressed grapeseed or canola oil
- 1¼ pounds (570 g) thick-cut boneless pork chops, trimmed, cut into 1¼-inch (3 cm) chunks*
- 2½ cups (275 g) whole bite-size potatoes, such as creamers
- 1 (8-ounce, or 225 g) package crimini (baby bella) mushrooms (about 2½ cups)
- 25 cherry tomatoes
- Your favorite meat dipping sauce

Preheat grill to medium heat, about 350°F (180°C, or gas mark 4). Whisk together amino acids, mustard, vinegar, rosemary, Worcestershire sauce, pepper, and garlic. Drizzle in the oil while stirring. Skewer the pork; place skewers on a sheet pan and drizzle half of the marinade over the meat. Turn skewers a few times to coat the meat completely; set aside. Place potatoes in a grill basket and toss with half of the remaining marinade. Place basket on the grill to cook potatoes 10 minutes prior to cooking pork and vegetables. Skewer the mushrooms and tomatoes and drizzle them with remaining marinade.

Oil the grill and place pork skewers at an angle on the hottest part of grate. Close the grill lid and cook for 5 minutes. Place mushroom and tomato skewers on cooler areas of the grill, turn the pork, and stir the potatoes. Brush vegetable and meat skewers with any marinade remaining in the pan. Close the grill lid and cook for 5 minutes until pork is done** and vegetables are tender, turning the vegetables halfway through. Enjoy with your favorite dipping sauce.

GO CLEAN

Condiments vary drastically in sodium and added sugar contents. Look for one that relies on ingredients that are flavorful in their own right with fruit and vegetable purées, garlic, herbs, and spices rather than those that rely on excessive amounts of added salt and refined sugar.

RECIPE NOTES

» *If only thin-cut pork chops are available, stack 2 pork chops on top of each other before cutting and tightly skewer 2 pieces together to form a thick chunk.

» Marinade that came into contact with raw meat can be used again in the cooking process as long as it is boiled or cooked at 165°F (74°C) for at least 15 seconds.

» **In 2011, the U.S. Department of Agriculture (USDA) announced that whole cuts of pork, such as pork chops, can be safely cooked to 145°F (63°C), followed by a 3-minute rest period. This equates to medium or medium-rare with a pink center. I was very happy about this news, since this practice results in juicier, tastier pork.

TOTAL PREP AND COOK TIME: 35 MINUTES • YIELD: 4 SERVINGS, 3 OUNCES (85 G) PORK EACH (WITH 1 CUP [APPROX. 125 G] VEGETABLES)

PER SERVING: 258 CALORIES; 12 G TOTAL FAT; 3 G SATURATED FAT; 21 G PROTEIN; 13 G CARBOHYDRATE; 2 G DIETARY FIBER; 57 MG CHOLESTEROL.

HERBED PORK MEDALLIONS WITH SAGE APPLE COMPOTE

The tart apples perfectly balance the sauce, resulting in a savory, not sweet, complement to the pork.

FOR PORK:

2 tablespoons (15 g) whole-wheat flour
½ teaspoon garlic powder
¼ teaspoon salt
¼ teaspoon freshly ground black pepper
2 teaspoons (4 g) Italian herb seasoning
1 pork tenderloin (about 1¼ pound, or 570 g), sliced crosswise into ¾-inch (2 cm)-thick medallions
2 tablespoons (28 ml) expeller-pressed grapeseed or canola oil

FOR COMPOTE:

½ small red onion, diced ¼ inch, or 6 mm (about ½ cup, or 80 g)
1 Granny Smith apple, peeled, cored, diced ¼ inch (6 mm)
1 celery stalk, diced ¼ inch, or 6 mm (about ½ cup, or 60 g)
1½ teaspoons (7.5 ml) apple cider vinegar
½ cup (120 ml) dry white wine, such as Chardonnay (or chicken broth)
¼ teaspoon ground sage
¼ teaspoon ground ginger
¼ teaspoon Italian herb seasoning
1 tablespoon (14 g) butter
¼ teaspoon salt
¼ teaspoon freshly ground black pepper
2 tablespoons (2 g) inner yellow celery leaves to garnish

TO MAKE THE PORK: Stir together flour, garlic powder, salt, pepper, and Italian seasoning in a shallow dish. Arrange the pork flat on a cutting board, pound it with a mallet to ½-inch (1.3 cm) thickness, and coat it in the seasoned flour on all sides. Heat a large skillet over medium heat and pour in 1 tablespoon (15 ml) of oil. When oil begins to shimmer, add pork in a single layer; you may need to divide the pork into 2 batches to avoid overcrowding the pan. Brown the pork on one side for 2 to 3 minutes; then turn to brown on the other side. Move the pork to a plate; using a wooden spoon, scrape the brown bits from the bottom of the pan and add them to the measured wine. Put the additional 2 teaspoons (10 ml) of oil into the pan and brown the remaining pork. Transfer the pork to the plate.

TO MAKE THE COMPOTE: Reduce heat to low and add onion, apple, celery, and vinegar and lightly sauté for 4 minutes to release the juices, using a wooden spoon to scrape the brown bits up from the bottom of the skillet. Add wine, sage, ginger, and Italian seasoning and cook over medium until the liquid has almost completely evaporated, about 6 minutes. Remove the skillet from the heat and swirl in butter, salt, and pepper. Spoon the compote onto plates and arrange pork slices on top. Sprinkle celery leaves on top of the pork.

 RECIPE NOTE

Instead of discarding leaves from produce, use those that are edible as flavorful garnishes, as in this dish. Fresh fennel leaves pair well with salads and fish, and sautéed beet greens make a tasty side dish.

 TOTAL PREP AND COOK TIME: 30 MINUTES • YIELD: 4 SERVINGS, 3 MEDALLIONS EACH (WITH ¼ CUP [APPROX. 76 G] COMPOTE)

PER SERVING: 274 CALORIES; 12 G TOTAL FAT; 3 G SATURATED FAT; 21 G PROTEIN; 18 G CARBOHYDRATE; 2 G DIETARY FIBER; 59 MG CHOLESTEROL.

HOISIN BEEF & EDAMAME LETTUCE WRAPS IN A HURRY

This is one of my signature dishes. I've honed and served it throughout my cooking career as a personal chef, newlywed, and mom. I present to you the simplest, most flavorful version yet. Feel free to substitute ground chicken, lean pork, or bison for the beef.

FOR SAUCE:

2 tablespoons (28 ml) reduced sodium soy sauce
1 tablespoon (16 g) hoisin sauce
1 tablespoon (15 ml) rice vinegar
2 teaspoons (8 g) Chinese mustard
1 teaspoon (7 g) honey
¼ teaspoon freshly ground black pepper

FOR BEEF:

1 tablespoon (15 ml) expeller-pressed grapeseed or canola oil
1 pound (455 g) organic or grass-fed ground beef
¼ teaspoon freshly ground black pepper
1 small onion, diced small (about 1 cup, or 160 g)
1 tablespoon (10 g) minced garlic
1 tablespoon (8 g) sesame seeds
2 teaspoons (4 g) minced ginger
1 cup (118 g) frozen shelled edamame, partially thawed (or peas)
1 (8-ounce, or 225 g) can sliced water chestnuts, drained, roughly chopped
½ cup (55 g) shredded carrots

FOR ASSEMBLY:

1 head Bibb, butter, or iceberg lettuce, separated into individual cups
Cooked brown rice
Reduced sodium soy sauce, Sriracha chili sauce, and peanut sauce for drizzling

TO MAKE THE SAUCE: In a small bowl, stir together all the sauce ingredients and set aside.

TO MAKE THE BEEF: Heat a large wok or frying pan over high heat and pour in the oil. When oil begins to shimmer, add beef in a single layer and break into pieces. Sprinkle in the pepper and allow the beef to cook undisturbed for 5 minutes to brown. Then turn the beef; break it into smaller pieces, add onion, and brown for a few more minutes. If needed, add a splash of water to the pan and use a wooden spoon to scrape up any brown bits from the bottom of the pan. Reduce heat to medium. Push meat to one side of the pan, add garlic, sesame seeds, and ginger to the other side, and cook until sesame seeds turn golden, about 20 seconds. Add edamame, water chestnuts, and carrots and stir-fry for 4 more minutes until vegetables become tender.

Swirl the sauce into the beef and stir-fry for 1 minute.

TO ASSEMBLE: Serve hot over cool lettuce cups with sauces spooned over the top and rice served on the side.

 GO CLEAN

Grapeseed oil has a light, neutral taste and can be heated to higher temperatures than most oils, making it perfect for stir-fries. Look for "expeller-pressed" varieties, which rely on mechanical extraction with a small amount of heat instead of chemicals.

TOTAL PREP AND COOK TIME: 45 MINUTES • YIELD: 4 SERVINGS, 1 CUP (APPROX. 249 G) BEEF FILLING EACH (WITH 3 LETTUCE CUPS)

PER SERVING (NOT INCLUDING BROWN RICE): 374 CALORIES; 20 G TOTAL FAT; 6 G SATURATED FAT; 29 G PROTEIN; 19 G CARBOHYDRATE; 5 G DIETARY FIBER; 70 MG CHOLESTEROL.

BEEF & BELL PEPPER STROGANOFF WITH WHOLE-WHEAT NOODLES

Greek yogurt replaces sour cream in this classic dish, and the addition of bell pepper provides vegetables, making it a nutritious all-in-one meal.

1 tablespoon + 2 teaspoons (25 ml) expeller-pressed grapeseed or canola oil, divided

1 pound (455 g) flank steak, or another tender cut of beef, thinly sliced against the grain into strips

1½ teaspoons (3.8 g) paprika

½ teaspoon salt, divided

¼ teaspoon freshly ground black pepper, divided

1 (8-ounce, or 225 g) package crimini (baby bella) mushrooms, thickly sliced (about 2½ cups)

1 medium red bell pepper, diced ½ inch (1.3 cm)

¾ cup (120 g) thinly sliced red onion

½ cup (120 ml) dry red wine

1 cup (235 ml) organic beef broth

½ cup (115 g) nonfat plain Greek yogurt

2 teaspoons (10 g) Dijon mustard

5 cups (700 g) cooked whole-wheat egg noodles or 4 cups (195 g) cooked brown rice, hot

3 tablespoons (12 g) chopped parsley

Heat a large skillet over high heat and add 2 teaspoons (10 ml) of the oil. Add beef in a single layer and sprinkle with paprika, ¼ teaspoon of salt, and ⅛ teaspoon of pepper. Brown for 4 minutes and add 2 tablespoons (28 ml) of water at the end, using a wooden spoon to scrape any brown bits from the bottom of the pan. Transfer beef to a plate. Place back on medium heat and add remaining tablespoon (15 ml) of oil. When oil begins to shimmer, add mushrooms, bell pepper, and onion and sauté until tender, about 7 minutes, reducing heat as vegetables shrink. Add wine and simmer until mostly evaporated, about 2 minutes. Add broth and reduce by half. Add cooked meat back to the pan to reheat. Remove the pan from the heat for 1 minute and stir in yogurt and mustard (removing the pan from the heat prevents the yogurt from curdling).

Serve the stroganoff over the cooked noodles, sprinkle with parsley, and enjoy hot.

 GO CLEAN

Mushrooms are a rich source of umami, one of the five basic tastes, providing a pleasant savory flavor imparted by the amino acid glutamate, among other naturally occurring compounds. The firm texture and full-bodied taste of cremini mushrooms blend in with beef, fooling your taste buds into thinking you're eating more meat, but with fewer calories and saturated fat grams.

TOTAL PREP AND COOK TIME: 35 MINUTES • YIELD: 5 SERVINGS, 1½ CUPS (APPROX. 323 G) EACH

PER SERVING: 347 CALORIES; 9 G TOTAL FAT; 2 G SATURATED FAT; 28 G PROTEIN; 37 G CARBOHYDRATE; 6 G DIETARY FIBER; 50 MG CHOLESTEROL.

CHAPTER 5

HEARTY MEATLESS MEALS

HEARTY PINTO & KIDNEY BEAN TAMALE PIE

Half chili, half cornbread, this dish is satisfying and delicious. Feel free to use cornbread mix as a shortcut, with enough batter for six muffins being the ideal amount to pour on top.

FOR FILLING:

1 tablespoon (15 ml) expeller-pressed grapeseed or canola oil
1 small onion, finely diced (about 1 cup, or 160 g)
2 teaspoons (6 g) minced garlic
1 (15-ounce, or 425 g) can pinto beans, rinsed and drained
1 (15-ounce, or 425 g) can kidney beans, rinsed and drained
1 (14.5-ounce, or 390 g) can diced tomatoes with green pepper, celery, and onion
2 teaspoons (5 g) chili powder
2 tablespoons (28 ml) lime juice
2 tablespoons (28 ml) reduced sodium soy sauce
¼ teaspoon freshly ground black pepper

FOR TOPPING:

½ cup (70 g) whole-grain corn flour or fine-ground whole-grain cornmeal
½ cup (60 g) whole-wheat pastry flour (or white whole-wheat flour)
2 teaspoons (9 g) baking powder
¼ teaspoon salt
½ cup (120 ml) low-fat milk
1 large egg
3 tablespoons (45 ml) canola oil
1½ teaspoons (10 g) light agave nectar
Garnishes: salsa, plain Greek yogurt, and avocado slices

Preheat oven to 425°F (220°C, or gas mark 7).

TO MAKE THE FILLING: Heat a large skillet over medium-low heat and add oil. When oil begins to shimmer, add onion and garlic and cook until translucent, about 4 minutes. Add beans, tomatoes, chili powder, lime juice, soy sauce, and pepper and stir, cooking until hot. Spread evenly into a 9 x 9-inch (23 x 23 cm) baking dish.

TO MAKE THE TOPPING: Stir together flours, baking powder, and salt in a medium bowl. Combine milk, egg, oil, and agave nectar in a small bowl. Add the wet ingredients to the dry ingredients and stir just until moistened. Pour batter over filling and spread evenly, manipulating as little as possible to avoid overworking. Bake until lightly golden and a toothpick inserted into the center comes out clean, about 20 minutes. Allow to rest for 5 minutes and then cut into 6 servings. Serve with salsa, yogurt, or avocado toppings.

 GO CLEAN

Whole-grain corn flour or cornmeal includes the germ, giving it 4 to 5 grams of fiber per serving, versus just 2 grams in "enriched and degerminated" varieties.

TOTAL PREP AND COOK TIME: 50 MINUTES • YIELD: 6 SERVINGS, 1 PIECE EACH

PER SERVING: 320 CALORIES; 11 G TOTAL FAT; 1 G SATURATED FAT; 13 G PROTEIN; 38 G CARBOHYDRATE; 8G DIETARY FIBER; 2 MG CHOLESTEROL.

QUICK POLENTA GRIDDLE CAKES WITH WILD MUSHROOM & CHERRY TOMATO SAUTÉ

This dish looks and tastes like something from a fancy menu, but it takes only 30 minutes to prepare from start to finish. My secret? I use "heat and serve" polenta, which is ready in a few minutes, instead of cooking cornmeal from scratch, with the lengthy boil-chill steps required.

FOR POLENTA:

2 tablespoons (28 ml) extra-virgin olive oil, divided

2 tablespoons (15 g) chickpea (garbanzo bean) flour (or whole-wheat flour)

¼ teaspoon salt

¼ teaspoon freshly ground black pepper

1 (18-ounce, or 510 g) sleeve precooked polenta, cut into eight ½-inch (1.3 cm) slices

FOR MUSHROOMS:

2 teaspoons (10 ml) extra-virgin olive oil

1 (8-ounce, or 225 g) package crimini (baby bella) mushrooms, thickly sliced (about 2½ cups)

1 (5-ounce, or 140 g) package shiitake mushrooms, stemmed and quartered

3 fresh thyme branches

1 tablespoon (10 g) minced garlic

2 tablespoons (28 ml) organic or reduced sodium vegetable broth

1½ cups (225 g) halved cherry tomatoes

¼ teaspoon salt

¼ teaspoon freshly ground black pepper

3 tablespoons (45 g) nonfat plain Greek yogurt

3 tablespoons (15 g) grated Parmesan cheese

TO MAKE THE POLENTA: Heat a large frying pan over medium heat and add 1 tablespoon (15 ml) of oil. In a shallow dish, stir together flour, salt, and pepper. Coat polenta circles in flour on all sides and gently tap each one against the side of the dish to remove excess flour. When oil begins to shimmer, carefully add polenta, sliding the pieces into the pan in a single layer, angling them away from you to minimize the risk of hot oil splattering. Cook for 5 minutes until golden on one side, gently shaking the pan occasionally. Turn the pieces of polenta over, drizzle in 1 tablespoon (15 ml) of oil between each piece, and brown for 4 minutes. Remove the polenta from the pan and place it on a plate; keep warm.

TO MAKE THE MUSHROOMS: Place the pan back on medium heat and add oil. Add mushrooms, thyme sprigs, and garlic and sauté until tender, about 4 minutes. Pour in the broth and use a wooden spoon to scrape up any brown bits from the bottom of the pan. Add tomatoes, salt, and pepper and cook until slightly softened, about 2 minutes. Remove the pan from the heat and discard the whole thyme sprigs. Stir in the yogurt and Parmesan cheese.

Serve the mushrooms over the polenta and enjoy hot.

 RECIPE NOTE

I created this recipe using "original" flavor polenta; however, you may also find it available in Italian herb and sun-dried tomato flavors. Choose whichever suits your palate and adjust seasoning accordingly.

 TOTAL PREP AND COOK TIME: 30 MINUTES • YIELD: 4 SERVINGS, 2 PIECES POLENTA EACH (WITH ½ CUP [APPROX. 165 G] VEGETABLES)

PER SERVING: 503 CALORIES; 11 G TOTAL FAT; 2 G SATURATED FAT; 15 G PROTEIN; 87 G CARBOHYDRATE; 10 G DIETARY FIBER; 5 MG CHOLESTEROL.

SLOW COOKER CUMIN BLACK BEANS & BROWN RICE

This classic Cuban dish is easily prepared in a slow cooker and delivers a complex depth of taste.

2 (15-ounce, or 425 g) cans black beans, one can rinsed and drained, one can undrained

1 cup (160 g) diced red onion

1 small green bell pepper, diced ½ inch (1.3 cm) (about 1⅓ cups, or 200 g)

2 tablespoons (28 ml) extra-virgin olive oil

1 tablespoon (10 g) minced garlic

½ teaspoon grated lime zest

1 tablespoon (15 ml) freshly squeezed lime juice

2 teaspoons (5 g) ground cumin

½ teaspoon salt

½ teaspoon freshly ground black pepper

½ teaspoon dried oregano leaves

½ teaspoon hot sauce

2 bay leaves

2 cups (390 g) cooked brown rice

3 tablespoons (12 g) chopped parsley

In a slow cooker, combine beans, onion, bell pepper, oil, garlic, lime zest and juice, cumin, salt, pepper, oregano, hot sauce, and bay leaves. Cover and cook on low for 4 hours. At the end of cooking, purée 1 cup (172 g) of the mixture and add back to the beans. Serve in bowls over rice and sprinkle with parsley.

 RECIPE NOTES

Rather than having to break out the full-size blender from your cabinet, you can plunge the immersion (or stick) blender head directly into the pot to purée. Hold the blender steady on one side to blend just a portion of the recipe. The immersion blender is another time-saving device that takes up minimal space, requires washing only one piece, and comes in handy for smoothies, sauces, and soups.

TOTAL PREP AND COOK TIME: 4½ HOURS • YIELD: 4 SERVINGS, ROUNDED ¾ CUP (129 G) BEANS AND ½ CUP (98 G) RICE EACH

PER SERVING: 382 CALORIES; 9 G TOTAL FAT; 1 G SATURATED FAT; 15 G PROTEIN; 63 G CARBOHYDRATE; 15 G DIETARY FIBER; 0 MG CHOLESTEROL.

WHOLE-WHEAT FARFALLE WITH FRESH MOZZARELLA TOMATO SAUCE

I learned how to make this dish in a cooking class in Lucca, Italy, at Chef Paolo Monti's Cucina Italiana. Making it transports me back to that magical wedding anniversary vacation. The basic tomato sauce can be used anytime you need a quick pasta sauce. If you wish to make this dish more substantial, stir in cooked chickpeas, chicken, or mushrooms.

5 cups (700 g) cooked whole-grain farfalle (bowtie) pasta (approximately 2½ cups dry, or 20 ounces [280 g])

2 tablespoons (28 ml) extra-virgin olive oil

1 tablespoon (10 g) minced garlic

1 pinch red pepper flakes

1 (28-ounce, or 785 g) can whole tomatoes, drained, skins and spots discarded

5 basil leaves (or ½ teaspoon dried basil leaves) + tiny leaves for garnishing

½ teaspoon honey

½ teaspoon salt

½ teaspoon freshly ground black pepper

5 ounces (140 g) fresh mozzarella cheese, chopped (1 heaping cup)

¼ cup (25 g) grated Parmesan cheese

Cook pasta according to package directions and keep warm.

Heat a medium saucepan over medium heat and add oil. Add garlic and chile flakes and cook until tender and aromatic, about 30 seconds. Using your hands, break up the tomatoes by squeezing them over the saucepan and allowing them to fall in. Add basil and simmer on medium-low for 10 minutes. Remove saucepan from heat and stir in the honey, salt, and pepper. Allow to cool for 2 minutes until warm, not hot. Discard the basil leaves.

Place warm sauce and mozzarella in a blender and purée until smooth. Reheat pasta and sauce in the saucepan over low heat; do not let it boil to avoid breaking the sauce. Garnish with basil leaves and Parmesan cheese.

 RECIPE NOTE

You can substitute 1¼ cups (145 g) of shredded block mozzarella for fresh.

 GO GREEN

Italian-imported canned tomatoes are expensive compared to domestic varieties and log many miles before they land in your pasta bowl. Further, a *Cook's Illustrated* detailed taste test revealed that two major domestic brands were better than the imports, and I agree.

 <30 TOTAL PREP AND COOK TIME: 30 MINUTES • YIELD: 4 SERVINGS, 1⅓ CUPS (APPROX. 419 G) EACH

PER SERVING: 502 CALORIES; 19 G TOTAL FAT; 6 G SATURATED FAT; 26 G PROTEIN; 59 G CARBOHYDRATE; 7 G DIETARY FIBER; 25 MG CHOLESTEROL.

WHOLE-WHEAT SPINACH RICOTTA CALZONES

These vegetable cheese pies are so satisfying and provide a fun switch up from pizza on the weekends. The dough formula stems from one of my favorite magazines, *Cook's Illustrated*.

FOR DOUGH:

1½ cups (355 ml) warm water (105°F to 110°F [41°C to 43°C])
1 (¾-ounce, or 20 g) envelope quick-acting dry yeast
2 cups (240 g) unbleached white whole-wheat flour, plus additional for dusting
2 cups (274 g) unbleached bread flour
¼ cup (60 ml) extra-virgin olive oil, divided
1½ teaspoons (9 g) salt
1½ teaspoons (3 g) Italian herb seasoning
Olive oil spray

FOR FILLING:

1 tablespoon (15 ml) extra-virgin olive oil
1 (8-ounce, or 225 g) package crimini (baby bella) mushrooms, finely chopped
4 cups (120 g) lightly packed baby spinach, finely chopped
2 teaspoons (6 g) minced garlic
½ cup (136 g) soft goat cheese
1 cup (250 g) whole milk ricotta cheese
¼ cup (25 g) grated Parmesan cheese
½ cup (20 g) basil leaves, chopped small
¼ cup (28 g) drained sun-dried tomatoes in oil, chopped
1 tablespoon (7 g) flaxseed meal
¼ teaspoon salt
¼ teaspoon freshly ground black pepper

FOR SERVING:

1⅓ cups (333 g) marinara sauce

TO MAKE THE DOUGH: Pour the water into the bowl of a stand mixer fitted with a dough hook, sprinkle in the yeast, and let it sit for 5 minutes. Add the flours, 3 tablespoons (45 ml) of oil, and salt and seasoning and mix for 10 minutes on medium-low speed until dough is elastic in consistency. Cover the bowl tightly with plastic wrap and place it in a warm area until the dough doubles in size, about 90 minutes. If you don't have a warm area in your kitchen, heat the oven to 200°F (93°C). Turn off the oven and wait 5 minutes before placing the dough in the oven to proof.

Once dough has risen, punch down. Coat a large sheet pan (or 2 medium sheets) with olive oil spray, shape the dough into 7 equal balls, cover, and let rest for 15 minutes.

TO MAKE THE FILLING: Heat a large frying pan over medium heat and add oil. When oil begins to shimmer, add mushrooms and sauté for 3 minutes; add spinach and garlic and cook until water releases and evaporates. Remove pan from heat and stir in the goat cheese. Add ricotta, Parmesan cheese, basil, tomatoes, flaxseed meal, salt, and pepper and stir. Transfer to a container and chill.

TO ASSEMBLE A CALZONE: Preheat oven to 500°F (250°C, or gas mark 10). Dust the counter, rolling pin, and a dough ball with flour. Flatten the dough into a 5-inch (13 cm) circle, rotating after every few rolls. Place ⅓ cup (85 g) of filling on the front half of the dough, leaving ½ inch (1.3 cm) around the border. Fold the dough over until the edges meet, forming a half-moon. Fold over ½ inch (1.3 cm). Press the edges with your fingers to seal and score lightly with a fork. Gently, but quickly, transfer the calzone back to the sheet pan. Repeat this process with the remaining dough and filling. Brush the calzones with 1 tablespoon (15 ml) of oil and using kitchen shears, cut four ½-inch (1.3 cm) slits into the tops of each. Bake on the middle rack until lightly golden on top and bottom, 15 to 18 minutes.

TO SERVE: Complement with warm marinara sauce.

TOTAL PREP AND COOK TIME: 1 HOUR, PLUS PROOFING TIME • YIELD: 7 SERVINGS, 1 CALZONE EACH (WITH 3 TABLESPOONS [45 G] MARINARA SAUCE)

PER SERVING: 614 CALORIES; 28 G TOTAL FAT; 10 G SATURATED FAT; 25 G PROTEIN; 64 G CARBOHYDRATE; 8 G DIETARY FIBER; 37 MG CHOLESTEROL.

BUCKWHEAT NOODLE BOWL WITH EDAMAME & GINGER

Get your Zen on with this Japanese-inspired dish. Your well-stocked "clean" kitchen will likely have all of these ingredients on hand for a quick, one-pot dinner.

1 tablespoon (15 ml) expeller-pressed grapeseed or canola oil

2 medium carrots, coarsely shredded (about 2 cups, or 220 g)

4 scallions, green parts diagonally cut into ¼-inch [6 mm] pieces, white parts chopped, divided

5 thin slices peeled gingerroot

2 cloves garlic, smashed

5 cups (1.2 L) organic or reduced sodium vegetable broth

2 (3.5-ounce, or 100 g) bundles dry buckwheat (soba) noodles

1¼ cups (148 g) frozen shelled edamame

1 sheet roasted nori (optional, found in Asian food section), cut into bite-size strips

1 tablespoon + 2 teaspoons (25 ml) tamari (or soy sauce)

Heat a large pot over medium heat and add oil. When oil begins to shimmer, add carrots, white parts of scallions, gingerroot and garlic and stir-fry for 3 minutes. Pour in the broth and bring to a boil on high heat. Add noodles and bring back to a boil. Add edamame and maintain a low boil for 5 minutes until noodles are *al dente*. Stir in the nori and tamari.

 RECIPE NOTES

» When reheating leftovers, pour in a bit more broth for a soupy consistency.

» You can get away with using only 4 cups (1 L) of broth if you'd like the finished dish to have a thicker consistency.

 GO CLEAN

» Tamari is rich tasting, comparable to dark Chinese soy sauce, and it requires little or no wheat during the fermentation of soybeans.

» Buckwheat is actually an herb, with (surprisingly) no relation to wheat, and buckwheat noodles contain 3 grams of fiber per serving.

 TOTAL PREP AND COOK TIME: 30 MINUTES • YIELD: 4 SERVINGS, 1½ CUPS (APPROX. 450 G) EACH

PER SERVING: 300 CALORIES; 6 G TOTAL FAT; TRACE SATURATED FAT; 12 G PROTEIN; 53 G CARBOHYDRATE; 8 G DIETARY FIBER; 0 MG CHOLESTEROL.

RATATOUILLE PASTA WITH CHICKPEAS

This comforting yet light Italian dish offers familiar flavors and showcases seasonal produce during summer and early fall. My friend and colleague Lynn Ladd, who is also a registered dietitian, turned testing this into a family event by watching the cartoon movie *Ratatouille* while preparing the recipe. Her kids loved this activity—even her eighteen-month-old gobbled up the dish! Brilliant.

3 tablespoons (45 ml) extra-virgin olive oil, divided

1 small eggplant, diced ¾ inch or 2 cm (about 5½ cups, or 450 g)

1 red bell pepper, cut into strips (about 2 cups, or 300 g)

1 small zucchini, diced into ½-inch (1.3 cm) cubes (about 1½ cups, or 180 g)

1 small yellow squash, diced into ½-inch (1.3 cm) cubes (about 1½ cups, or 180 g)

1 small onion, diced into ½-inch (1.3 cm) cubes (about 1 cup, or 160 g)

1 tablespoon (10 g) minced garlic

1 (15-ounce, or 425 g) can puréed or crushed tomatoes

1 (15-ounce, or 425 g) can chickpeas, rinsed and drained

1 tablespoon (5 g) nutritional yeast seasoning (optional)

1 teaspoon (1 g) dried basil

½ teaspoon dried thyme

½ teaspoon salt

½ teaspoon freshly ground black pepper

4½ cups (630 g) cooked whole-grain fettuccine, hot, ½ cup (120 ml) cooking liquid reserved

⅓ cup (33 g) grated Parmesan cheese

Heat a large skillet over medium-high heat and add 1 table-spoon (15 ml) of oil. When oil begins to shimmer, add egg-plant, bell pepper, zucchini, and squash; stir and allow to cook undisturbed for 4 minutes to brown. Brown 5 more minutes, stirring occasionally. Add a splash of water and use a wooden spoon to scrape up any brown bits from the bottom of the pan. Reduce heat to medium-low and push vegetables to one side of the pan. Add 1 tablespoon (15 ml) of oil, along with onion and garlic, to other side of the pan and cook until tender, about 5 minutes. Add remaining oil to the pan and then add tomatoes, chickpeas, yeast seasoning, basil, thyme, salt, and pepper; stir together and simmer for 20 to 30 minutes to blend the flavors.

Toss the vegetables with the pasta and reserved liquid. Sprinkle each serving with Parmesan cheese.

 GO CLEAN

Nutritional yeast seasoning adds a savory umami and cheese-like flavor that vegan and vegetarian dishes might otherwise lack. Sprinkle yeast seasoning into soups, dips, and entrées, and over popcorn. It's sodium-free, and 1 tablespoon (5 g) adds 1 gram of fiber, 2 grams of protein, minerals, B vitamins, and only 20 calories. Find it in the natural food section near the spices.

TOTAL PREP AND COOK TIME: 1 HOUR • YIELD: 6 SERVINGS, 1½ CUPS (APPROX. 319 G) EACH (WITH 2 SCANT TEASPOONS [3.3 G] PARMESAN)

PER SERVING: 386 CALORIES; 11 G TOTAL FAT; 2 G SATURATED FAT; 16 G PROTEIN; 57 G CARBOHYDRATE; 12 G DIETARY FIBER; 5 MG CHOLESTEROL.

GRIDDLED APPLE CHEDDAR SANDWICHES WITH FRESH HERBS

This quick lunchtime recipe will satisfy your craving for a grilled cheese sandwich, while adding a bit of sweetness, a dab of earthiness, and 100 percent deliciousness.

4 slices whole-wheat bread (sprouted grain preferred)

2 teaspoons (10 g) coarse ground mustard

4 thin sandwich-size slices Cheddar cheese (reduced fat preferred)

1 small Gala apple, cored and very thinly sliced into circles

1 teaspoon (7 g) honey

1 teaspoon (1 g) roughly chopped rosemary or thyme

⅔ cup (22 g) alfalfa sprouts

⅛ teaspoon freshly ground black pepper

Place oven rack on second highest shelf, about 3 inches (7.5 cm) under heating element, and preheat oven to a low broil. Place bread on a sheet pan in a single layer and broil until toasted on top, about 1½ minutes. Remove pan from oven.

Spread mustard on untoasted side of 2 slices of bread. Lay 2 pieces of cheese and half of the apple slices on each slice of bread and drizzle honey over the apples. Place the pan back in the oven and broil for 5 minutes until apples become tender. Remove the pan from the oven. Place rosemary and sprouts on top of the apple slices and sprinkle with pepper. Sandwich the other 2 slices of bread on top, toasted side up, and cut in half diagonally. Serve warm.

 TOTAL PREP AND COOK TIME: 15 MINUTES • YIELD: 2 SERVINGS, 1 SANDWICH EACH

PER SERVING: 490 CALORIES; 30 G TOTAL FAT; 13 G SATURATED FAT; 22 G PROTEIN; 34 G CARBOHYDRATE; 8 G DIETARY FIBER; 59 MG CHOLESTEROL.

OLIVE OIL–CURED SUMMER VEGETABLE SANDWICHES

When I was a caterer, one of my chefs whipped up these succulent vegetables for her own lunch, and they tasted so good that I immediately included them on the menu in a sandwich. They are a wonderful option for vegetarians and perfect for a road trip, sack lunch, or picnic, in which case you should allow the vegetables to cool prior to assembling. Steve loved these and didn't even miss the meat—a first.

1 medium zucchini, halved lengthwise, sliced on an angle into half-moons (about 2 cups, or 240 g)

1 medium yellow squash, halved lengthwise, sliced on an angle into half-moons (about 2½ cups, or 300 g)

1 (8-ounce, or 225 g) package cremini (baby bella) mushrooms, quartered (about 2½ cups)

1½ cups (225 g) halved cherry tomatoes

½ red onion, sliced into rings

2 tablespoons (28 ml) sherry vinegar (or balsamic)

1 tablespoon (15 g) Dijon mustard

1 teaspoon (7 g) honey

1 teaspoon (2 g) dried Italian herb seasoning

¼ teaspoon salt

¼ teaspoon freshly ground black pepper

2 tablespoons (28 ml) extra-virgin olive oil

¾ cup (185 g) hummus (original, olive, roasted red pepper, or garlic flavor)

4 medium oblong sandwich rolls, slit horizontally (whole-grain preferred)

4 sandwich-size slices reduced fat provolone or mozzarella cheese, cut in half

Preheat oven to 375°F (190°C, or gas mark 5) and line 2 large sheet pans with parchment paper or silicone baking mats. Arrange vegetables in a single layer on the pans. In a small bowl, whisk vinegar, mustard, honey, Italian seasoning, salt, and pepper and drizzle in the oil, whisking to emulsify. Drizzle evenly on the vegetables and toss to coat. Bake until tender, about 25 minutes.

Spread the insides of the buns with hummus. Layer the vegetables on top, finish with cheese, and top with remaining bun halves. Cut sandwiches in half crosswise and enjoy immediately or wrap tightly and chill until ready to eat, within 1 day.

 GO CLEAN

Before opting for enticingly exotic-sounding olive oils from a distant country, explore the options available near you. Olives tend to grow well in regions where wine grapes thrive.

TOTAL PREP AND COOK TIME: 45 MINUTES • YIELD: 4 SERVINGS, 1 SANDWICH EACH (WITH ¾ CUP [APPROX. 135 G] VEGETABLES)

PER SERVING: 466 CALORIES; 18 G TOTAL FAT; 5 G SATURATED FAT; 23 G PROTEIN; 55 G CARBOHYDRATE; 11 G DIETARY FIBER; 15 MG CHOLESTEROL.

 RECIPE NOTE

Try toasting the buns before assembling for added flavor and texture if you will be enjoying them immediately.

EDAMAME MUSHROOM SAUTÉ WITH ALMONDS & SUN-DRIED TOMATOES

Edamame, or young green soybeans, are wonderful eaten straight out of the pods, and I love them with Friday night sushi takeout. I buy shelled edamame for recipes to save prep time. My taste testers like the meaty texture of the mushrooms, making it substantial enough for a main course, yet light as a side dish.

1 tablespoon (15 ml) expeller-pressed grapeseed or canola oil

1 (8-ounce, or 225 g) package cremini (baby bella) mushrooms, thickly sliced (about 2½ cups)

1 pinch salt

1 cup (160 g) sliced red onion

1 teaspoon (3 g) minced garlic

1 (16-ounce, 3-cup, or 455 g) bag frozen shelled edamame soybeans, partially thawed

⅓ cup (80 ml) organic or reduced sodium vegetable broth

¼ cup (28 g) drained sun-dried tomatoes in oil, chopped

¼ cup (40 g) dried tart cherries, chopped

¼ cup (15 g) chopped parsley

2 teaspoons (10 ml) lemon juice

1 teaspoon (7 g) light agave nectar or honey

¼ teaspoon salt

¼ teaspoon freshly ground black pepper

¼ cup (28 g) sliced or chopped almonds, toasted

Heat 1 tablespoon (15 ml) of oil in a large frying pan over medium-high heat. When oil begins to shimmer, add mushrooms and pinch of salt and toss a few times to coat; stir occasionally and brown for 3 to 4 minutes, adding a splash of water at the end if needed to deglaze the brown bits from the bottom of the pan. Reduce heat to medium, add onion and garlic, and cook for 4 minutes. Add edamame and cook until tender, about 5 minutes, pouring in the broth halfway through. Add tomatoes, cherries, parsley, lemon, agave, salt, and pepper and cook until hot. Remove from heat and sprinkle with almonds. Serve hot or enjoy cold the next day for lunch.

 TOTAL PREP AND COOK TIME: 30 MINUTES • YIELD: 3 SERVINGS, 1⅓ CUPS (APPROX. 300 G) EACH

PER SERVING: 481 CALORIES; 22 G TOTAL FAT; 1 G SATURATED FAT; 21 G PROTEIN; 49 G CARBOHYDRATE; 12 G DIETARY FIBER; 0 MG CHOLESTEROL.

BASIL WHITE BEAN FRITTERS WITH CHIVE YOGURT DIP

Fry it and they will come. The magical basil and bean combination pairs perfectly, and ranch-style dipping sauce doesn't hurt either. You can serve these fritters alongside dip, stuff them into whole-grain pita pockets, or shape them into large patties and eat them on hamburger buns with arugula and dip.

FOR FRITTERS:

2 (15-ounce, or 425 g) cans great northern or cannellini beans, rinsed and
   drained
1¼ cups (200 g) finely diced onion
1 cup (120 g) whole-wheat flour
⅓ cup (77 g) nonfat plain Greek yogurt
16 large basil leaves, rolled and sliced into
   very thin strips (about ¼ cup, or 10 g,
   or 4 teaspoons [3 g] dried)
4 teaspoons (12 g) minced garlic
2 teaspoons (10 g) Dijon mustard
2 teaspoons (9 g) baking powder
2 teaspoons (10 ml) lemon juice
½ teaspoon salt
½ teaspoon freshly ground black pepper
¼ cup (60 ml) extra-virgin olive oil,
   divided

FOR DIP:

¼ cup (60 g) nonfat plain Greek yogurt
¼ cup (60 g) light mayonnaise
1 tablespoon (3 g) chopped chives
1 teaspoon (5 ml) lemon juice
¼ teaspoon garlic powder
1 pinch salt
1 pinch freshly ground black pepper

TO MAKE THE FRITTERS: Mash the beans in a medium bowl until chunky. Add onion, flour, yogurt, basil, garlic, mustard, baking powder, lemon juice, salt, and pepper and using your hands, knead the mixture in the bowl. Shape the mixture into sixteen 1¼-inch (3 cm) balls and flatten them slightly into patties. Heat a large skillet over medium heat and pour in 2 tablespoons (28 ml) of oil. When oil begins to shimmer, add patties, in 2 batches, and brown for 4 minutes. Turn patties over; pour in 2 more tablespoons (28 ml) of oil and brown on the other sides. Put patties on a plate lined with a paper towel.

TO MAKE THE DIP: Stir together all the dip ingredients.

Serve the patties warm, with the dip.

 RECIPE NOTE

If you purchase a bunch of fresh basil, you can use the remaining basil in tomato cheese sandwiches, Italian cuisine, cucumber salad, or smoothies with peaches, oranges, or pineapple. Basil lasts only a few days refrigerated and is too good to waste!

 TOTAL PREP AND COOK TIME: 30 MINUTES • YIELD: 4 SERVINGS, 4 PATTIES AND 2 TABLESPOONS (28 G) DIP EACH

PER SERVING: 466 CALORIES; 19 G TOTAL FAT; 2 G SATURATED FAT; 19 G PROTEIN; 56 G CARBOHYDRATE; 13 G DIETARY FIBER; 7 MG CHOLESTEROL.

WINTER VEGETABLE BARLEY STEW WITH WHOLE-WHEAT POPOVERS

My grandma's light-as-air popovers are the perfect accompaniment the idea for this satisfying, hearty stew full of aromatic vegetables.

FOR STEW:
2 tablespoons (28 ml) extra-virgin olive oil
1 bunch kale, thick ribs removed, leaves chopped
1 medium leek, white part only, sliced thin (about 1½ cups, or 134 g)
1 head fennel, bulb quartered, core removed, sliced thin
½ teaspoon salt, divided
½ teaspoon freshly ground black pepper, divided
1 celery root, peeled, cubed into bite-size pieces (2¾ cups, or 429 g)
¾ cup (150 g) dry pearl barley
6 cups (1.5 L) organic or reduced sodium vegetable broth
3 tablespoons (15 g) nutritional yeast seasoning, plus additional for sprinkling (optional)
1 tablespoon (4 g) chopped fennel leaves (from top fennel bulb)
2 teaspoons (4 g) dried Italian herb seasoning

FOR POPOVERS:
Expeller-pressed canola oil spray
2 large eggs, room temperature
1 cup (235 ml) low-fat milk, room temperature
1 tablespoon (15 ml) expeller-pressed grapeseed or canola oil (or melted butter for richer taste)
¼ teaspoon salt (or ½ teaspoon if eaten plain without spread)
½ cup (60 g) white whole-wheat flour
½ cup (63 g) unbleached all-purpose flour

Preheat oven to 450°F (230°C, or gas mark 8).

TO MAKE THE STEW: Heat a large pot over medium heat and add oil. When oil begins to shimmer, add kale, leek, fennel, and ¼ teaspoon each of salt and pepper and sauté until tender, about 10 minutes, reducing heat as needed. Add celery root, barley, broth, and 1 cup (235 ml) of water and bring to a boil on high. Reduce heat to low and cover the pot, leaving the lid slightly ajar; simmer for 20 minutes until celery root smashes easily and is no longer bitter and barley is tender but still has "chew." Sprinkle in the yeast (for added flavor), fennel leaves, Italian seasoning, and remaining ¼ teaspoon each salt and pepper and stir.

TO MAKE THE POPOVERS: Coat a 12-muffin tin with canola oil spray. In a medium bowl, whisk eggs until frothy; then blend in milk, oil, and salt, sift in flours, and mix until smooth. Fill each tin halfway. Bake for 18 minutes until popovers are poufed and mostly browned; then reduce heat to 350°F (180°C, or gas mark 4) and bake for an additional 10 to 15 minutes until they are browned evenly. Cool the popovers until they are just firm enough that they can be removed from the pan without collapsing. Tear them open to release steam before biting into them.

 RECIPE NOTE

If you've never tried kale, here's your opportunity. Its dark green hue adds a nice contrast, and I crave its earthy cabbage flavor. If you prefer, you can substitute 4 cups (280 g) of shredded green cabbage.

TOTAL PREP AND COOK TIME: 1 HOUR • YIELD: 6 SERVINGS, 1¼ CUPS (APPROX. 170 G) STEW EACH (WITH 2 POPOVERS)

PER SERVING: 363 CALORIES; 10 G TOTAL FAT; 2 G SATURATED FAT; 12 G PROTEIN; 56 G CARBOHYDRATE; 11 G DIETARY FIBER; 65 MG CHOLESTEROL.

BROWN RICE RISOTTO WITH ASPARAGUS, ROASTED TOMATOES & ALMONDS

While the idea of making risotto might be intimidating at first, your worries will fade once you understand the proper way to prepare it.

2 tablespoons + 1 teaspoon (33 ml) extra-virgin olive oil, divided

1 small yellow onion, finely diced (about 1 cup, or 160 g)

1 cup (190 g) short-grain brown rice (found in natural food section)

¼ cup (60 ml) vermouth (or dry white wine)

6 cups (1.5 L) organic or reduced sodium vegetable broth, divided

1 bunch asparagus, woody bottom third cut off

1½ cups (225 g) halved cherry tomatoes

¼ teaspoon salt, divided

¼ teaspoon freshly ground white pepper or black pepper, divided

6 thyme sprigs (or ½ teaspoon dried thyme)

¼ cup (25 g) grated Parmesan cheese

¼ cup (60 g) nonfat plain Greek yogurt

1 tablespoon (14 g) cold butter, cubed

¼ cup (28 g) chopped or sliced almonds, toasted

Preheat oven to 375°F (190°C, or gas mark 5). Line a sheet pan with parchment paper or a silicone baking mat.

Heat a large skillet over medium-low heat and add 2 tablespoons (28 ml) of oil. Add onion and sauté until translucent, about 5 minutes. In a saucepan, heat broth on low. Add rice and cook for 7 minutes, stirring frequently, until edges are slightly browned and aromatic, reducing heat as needed.

Pour in the vermouth and simmer until almost evaporated. Pour in ¼ cup (60 ml) of broth, swirling the pan occasionally and scraping down the sides with a wooden spoon. Resist stirring to avoid crushing the rice and making it mushy. When broth has reduced to rice level, add another ¼ cup (60 ml) of broth and continue with this process for the next 30 minutes or so until the rice is al dente and creamy. You will probably use all of the broth. Risotto should be pourable, not sticky or firm.

Meanwhile, place asparagus and tomatoes on the lined baking sheet, cut side up. Drizzle with 1 teaspoon (5 ml) of oil, sprinkle ⅛ teaspoon each of salt and pepper, and lay thyme on top. Bake until tender, about 30 minutes, and reserve for finishing, cutting the asparagus into bite-size pieces.

Remove risotto from heat and stir in the asparagus, Parmesan cheese, yogurt, butter, and remaining salt and pepper. Spoon risotto into bowls and place warm tomatoes and almonds on top. Enjoy immediately.

GO GREEN

When adding the cheese, stir in ¼ cup (40 g) of dried tart cherries instead of tomatoes during winter months.

RECIPE NOTE

Use room-temperature broth from the carton or hot broth to speed cooking time.

TOTAL PREP AND COOK TIME: 1 HOUR • YIELD: 4 SERVINGS, 1 CUP (APPROX. 200 G) RISOTTO EACH (WITH 2 TABLESPOONS TOMATOES [22.5 G] AND 1 TABLESPOON [7 G] ALMONDS)

PER SERVING: 338 CALORIES; 17 G TOTAL FAT; 4 G SATURATED FAT; 9 G PROTEIN; 35 G CARBOHYDRATE; 6 G DIETARY FIBER; 14 MG CHOLESTEROL.

CHAPTER 6

QUICK
& TASTY
SIDE DISHES

◄ QUINOA PILAF WITH MIREPOIX

Mirepoix is French for the combination of onions, celery, and carrots and is used as a base in cooking to provide aromatic flavor.

1 cup (173 g) dry quinoa
1 tablespoon (15 ml) extra-virgin olive oil
1 carrot, diced small
½ small onion, diced small (about ½ cup, or 80 g)
1 celery stalk, diced small
1¾ cups (410 ml) organic or reduced sodium vegetable broth
½ teaspoon dried Italian herb seasoning
1 teaspoon (5 ml) apple cider vinegar
¼ teaspoon salt
¼ teaspoon freshly ground black pepper

In a medium saucepan, cover quinoa in water and allow it to soak for 5 minutes. Stir quinoa and pour into a strainer, rinse with cool water. Dry the saucepan, then heat it over medium heat and add oil. When oil begins to shimmer, add carrot, onion, and celery and cook until tender, about 4 minutes. Add quinoa and sauté until the mixture emits a nutty aroma, about 1 minute. Pour in the broth and bring to a boil on high. Reduce heat to low, add Italian seasoning, cover, and cook for 20 minutes until quinoa is tender and liquid is completely absorbed. Allow to sit covered for 5 minutes and then stir in the vinegar, salt, and pepper.

TOTAL PREP AND COOK TIME: 40 MINUTES • YIELD: 7 SERVINGS, ½ CUP (93 G) EACH

PER SERVING: 133 CALORIES; 3 G TOTAL FAT; TRACE SATURATED FAT; 4 G PROTEIN; 23 G CARBOHYDRATE; 3 G DIETARY FIBER; 0 MG CHOLESTEROL.

BROWN RICE WITH FRESH CILANTRO & LIME

This recipe serves as a pleasant, palate-cleansing side dish to accompany a rich Mexican- or Thai-themed meal.

1 cup (190 g) dry brown rice
1 tablespoon (15 ml) extra-virgin olive oil
1 scallion, thinly sliced, white and green parts, divided
2 teaspoons (6 g) minced garlic
1¾ cups (410 ml) organic or reduced sodium vegetable broth
1 lime, 1 teaspoon grated zest and 1 tablespoon (15 ml) juice
2 teaspoons (3 g) nutritional yeast seasoning (optional)
1 teaspoon (5 ml) liquid amino acids (or reduced sodium soy sauce)
3 tablespoons (3 g) chopped cilantro

Rinse and drain the rice. Heat a pot with a tight-fitting lid over medium-low heat and pour in the oil. When oil begins to shimmer, add the white parts of the scallion and the garlic and gently cook until aromatic, about 30 seconds. Add rice, broth, and lime zest and bring to a boil on high. Reduce heat to low, cover, and simmer until rice is tender and liquid is absorbed, about 40 minutes. Do not remove the lid while cooking. Remove from heat and allow rice to rest for 5 minutes. Add the green parts of the scallion, lime juice, nutritional yeast, amino acids, and cilantro, and fluff with a fork.

TOTAL PREP AND COOK TIME: 55 MINUTES, PLUS RESTING TIME • YIELD: 6 SERVINGS, ½ CUP (98 G) EACH

PER SERVING: 142 CALORIES; 3 G TOTAL FAT; TRACE SATURATED FAT; 2 G PROTEIN; 26 G CARBOHYDRATE; 1 G DIETARY FIBER; 0 MG CHOLESTEROL.

WEEKNIGHT WHOLE-GRAIN & WILD RICE PILAF

I love the taste and convenience of boxed whole-grain rice mixes, but I can do without the additives and high amounts of sodium, which is why I created this simple recipe. At the end of cooking, feel free to stir in chopped herbs or any leftover cooked vegetables you have on hand.

1 cup (160 g) dry whole-grain and wild rice blend (or brown rice)
1¾ cups (410 ml) organic or reduced sodium vegetable broth
1 tablespoon (15 ml) extra-virgin olive oil
1 tablespoon (5 g) nutritional yeast seasoning (optional)
1 teaspoon (2 g) Italian herb seasoning
1 teaspoon (2 g) dried onion flakes
½ teaspoon apple cider vinegar
¼ teaspoon garlic powder
¼ teaspoon freshly ground black pepper

Rinse and drain the rice. Place all the ingredients in a pot with a tight-fitting lid and bring to a boil on high heat. Reduce heat to low, cover, and simmer until rice is tender and liquid is absorbed, about 45 minutes. Do not lift the lid while cooking. Remove from heat and allow rice to rest for 5 minutes. Fluff with a fork.

TOTAL PREP AND COOK TIME: 50 MINUTES, PLUS RESTING TIME • YIELD: 5 SERVINGS, ½ CUP (98 G) EACH

PER SERVING: 161 CALORIES; 3 G TOTAL FAT; TRACE SATURATED FAT; 4 G PROTEIN; 28 G CARBOHYDRATE; 2 G DIETARY FIBER; 0 MG CHOLESTEROL.

BASIL-WALNUT MILLET PILAF

Chances are you've never cooked with millet, despite the fact that it ranks as the sixth most important cereal grain in the world. This ancient grain is gluten-free, is an excellent source of iron, ranks high in antioxidants, and contains more fiber and protein than brown rice. Look for it in the natural foods section.

¾ cup (150 g) dry millet
2¼ cups (535 ml) organic or reduced sodium vegetable broth
1 tablespoon (15 ml) extra-virgin olive oil
1 lemon, 1 teaspoon (5 ml) shredded zest and 1 teaspoon (2 g) juice, divided
¼ teaspoon garlic powder
¼ cup (10 g) thinly sliced basil leaves
¼ cup (30 g) chopped walnuts, toasted (or raw)
1 tablespoon (5 g) nutritional yeast seasoning (or grated Parmesan cheese)
¼ teaspoon salt
¼ teaspoon freshly ground black pepper

Combine millet, broth, oil, lemon zest, and garlic powder in a pot, cover, and bring to a boil on high. Reduce heat to low and simmer for 25 minutes. Allow to sit covered (don't peak!) for 10 minutes. Add lemon juice, basil, walnuts, nutritional yeast, salt, and pepper and fluff with a fork. Serve hot.

 TOTAL PREP AND COOK TIME: 40 MINUTES • YIELD: 8 SERVINGS, ½ CUP (APPROX. 93 G) EACH

PER SERVING: 106 CALORIES; 4 G TOTAL FAT; 1 G SATURATED FAT; 4 G PROTEIN; 14 G CARBOHYDRATE; 3 G DIETARY FIBER; 0 MG CHOLESTEROL.

MACARONI & CHEESY CAULIFLOWER SAUCE

"Mmmm . . . Yummy, yummy!" were Scarlet's words when she ate this. Scarlet was in the midst of a macaroni and cheese bender, so I decided it was time to sneak in some extra nutrition with this rendition that offers ¼ cup (25 g) of hidden cauliflower per serving.

2 cups (200 g) bite-size cauliflower florets

½ cup (120 ml) low-fat milk

1 cup (115 g) shredded sharp Cheddar cheese

⅓ cup (33 g) grated Parmesan cheese

½ teaspoon Dijon mustard

½ teaspoon garlic powder

¼ teaspoon onion powder

½ teaspoon paprika or turmeric (for color)

¼ + ⅛ teaspoon salt

1 pinch freshly ground white pepper (or ⅛ teaspoon black pepper)

5 cups (700 g) cooked whole-grain elbow macaroni, hot

¼ cup (60 g) plain low-fat yogurt

Fill a pot with 2 inches (5 cm) of water and insert a steamer basket. Add cauliflower and bring to a low boil. Cover and cook for 8 minutes until inner stem is fork-tender. Meanwhile, microwave milk until steamy.

Place cauliflower, hot milk (not boiling), cheeses, mustard, garlic powder, onion powder, paprika, salt, and pepper in a blender and purée until smooth. Combine pasta and cheese sauce in the empty pot used to cook the cauliflower and stir in yogurt.

 RECIPE NOTE

If you don't have a steamer basket, cook the cauliflower directly in the water, stirring occasionally to cook evenly. Or, you can microwave the cauliflower for 5 minutes, adding a splash of water, in a loosely covered dish.

 GO GREEN

Cauliflower is a cool-season crop, making fall and winter the peak time to enjoy this cruciferous vegetable. Fresh cauliflower available during spring and summer was likely grown in a greenhouse or hotbed.

 TOTAL PREP AND COOK TIME: 30 MINUTES • YIELD: 8 SERVINGS, ½ CUP (APPROX. 123 G) EACH

PER SERVING: 212 CALORIES; 6 G TOTAL FAT; 3 G SATURATED FAT; 12 G PROTEIN; 26 G CARBOHYDRATE; 3 G DIETARY FIBER; 17 MG CHOLESTEROL.

◄ROSEMARY SWEET POTATO OVEN FRIES WITH SPICY AIOLI

I finally discovered the perfect dipping sauce for sweet potatoes in France, where the French dip traditional fries in mayonnaise instead of ketchup.

FOR FRIES:

Expeller-pressed canola oil spray

2 sweet potatoes, peeled, cut lengthwise into long batons (like French fries)

1 tablespoon + 1 teaspoon (20 ml) expeller-pressed grapeseed or canola oil

2 teaspoons (2 g) chopped rosemary (or ¼ teaspoon dried thyme)

¼ teaspoon freshly ground black pepper

⅛ teaspoon salt

FOR AIOLI:

¼ cup (60 g) light olive oil mayonnaise (or plain light mayonnaise)

1 tablespoon (15 g) low-fat plain Greek yogurt

1 teaspoon (5 ml) lime juice

⅛ teaspoon curry powder

⅛ teaspoon garlic powder

Preheat oven to 450°F (230°C, or gas mark 8) and line a large sheet pan with a silicone baking mat or parchment paper coated with canola oil spray.

TO MAKE THE FRIES: Toss sweet potatoes with oil, rosemary, pepper, and salt and spread them out in a single layer on the sheet pan. Bake on the bottom rack of the oven until golden, about 30 minutes, turning them and rotating the pan after 15 minutes.

TO MAKE THE AIOLI: Stir together mayonnaise, yogurt, lime juice, curry powder, and garlic powder in a small bowl.

Serve the fries with the aioli.

TOTAL PREP AND COOK TIME: 45 MINUTES • YIELD: 4 SERVINGS, 12 FRIES EACH (WITH 1 ROUNDED TABLESPOON [14 G] AIOLI)

PER SERVING: 148 CALORIES; 9 G TOTAL FAT; TRACE SATURATED FAT; 1 G PROTEIN; 16 G CARBOHYDRATE; 2 G DIETARY FIBER; 5 MG CHOLESTEROL.

CARAMELIZED ACORN SQUASH WITH SAGE

Just a few simple ingredients add a zesty, earthy twist to this dish.

1 acorn squash, cut in half horizontally, seeds discarded

1 tablespoon (14 g) butter

1 orange, 1 teaspoon (2 g) grated zest and 2 tablespoons (28 ml) juice

2 teaspoons (13 g) real maple syrup

⅛ teaspoon salt

⅛ teaspoon freshly ground black pepper

1 teaspoon (1 g) dried sage

Preheat oven to 400°F (200°C, or gas mark 6) and line a sheet pan with parchment paper or a silicone baking mat. Place squash, cut side up, on the pan. Soften butter in microwave until almost melted (a few seconds) and stir in remaining ingredients, except sage. Coat inside of squash with the mixture. Bake until fork-tender and caramelized, about 35 minutes, depending on size, covering with foil toward the end of cooking to prevent squash from drying out. Sprinkle with sage. Cut pieces in half and serve in the skins or scoop out pulp and dish directly onto the plate. Enjoy hot.

TOTAL PREP AND COOK TIME: 45 MINUTES • YIELD: 4 SERVINGS, ¼ SQUASH EACH

PER SERVING: 82 CALORIES; 3 G TOTAL FAT; 2 G SATURATED FAT; 1 G PROTEIN; 14 G CARBOHYDRATE; 2 G DIETARY FIBER; 8 MG CHOLESTEROL.

GREEN BEANS WITH CARAMELIZED SHALLOTS & TARRAGON

There is life beyond plain steamed green beans, like in this recipe where vinegar adds brightness and shallots add a touch of caramelized sweetness.

2 teaspoons (10 ml) extra-virgin olive oil

2 medium shallots, thinly sliced into rings

3 cups (300 g) green beans, trimmed, cut in half crosswise

½ cup (120 ml) organic or reduced sodium vegetable broth

1 pinch salt

⅛ teaspoon freshly ground black pepper

¼ teaspoon dried tarragon (or 1 tablespoon [4 g] chopped fresh)

1 teaspoon (5 ml) red wine vinegar

Heat a large skillet over medium heat and add oil. When oil begins to shimmer, add shallots and sauté until wilted and light golden, about 15 minutes, reducing heat as needed and stirring occasionally. Add beans, broth, salt, and pepper and cover the pot with a lid, leaving space for steam to escape. Simmer on medium-low until tender, about 8 minutes. Sprinkle with tarragon during the final minute and finish with vinegar.

 GO GREEN

You can substitute frozen green beans for fresh during the off-season winter months. Frozen tiny green beans (haricots verts) are the prettiest.

TOTAL PREP AND COOK TIME: 30 MINUTES • YIELD: 5 SERVINGS, ½ CUP (APPROX. 70 G) EACH

PER SERVING: 42 CALORIES; 2 G TOTAL FAT; TRACE SATURATED FAT; 1 G PROTEIN; 6 G CARBOHYDRATE; 2 G DIETARY FIBER; 0 MG CHOLESTEROL.

PONZU KALE WITH GARLIC

There are times I simply crave the earthy, green taste of this dish. Ponzu sauce is sure to take me out of any flavor rut I might find myself in, with its notes of soy sauce, bonito (fish) flakes, and citrus. I recommend using it as you would soy sauce in Asian dishes.

1 tablespoon (15 ml) extra-virgin olive oil

2 teaspoons (6 g) minced garlic

I teaspoon (3 g) minced gingerroot

1 bunch kale, leaves cut off of ribs
   and chopped into bite-size pieces,
   ribs chopped small, divided

1 tablespoon (15 ml) ponzu sauce (found
   in Asian food section)

1 teaspoon (2 g) lemon zest

2 teaspoons (10 ml) organic or reduced-
   sodium vegetable broth

Heat a large skillet over medium heat and add oil. When oil begins to shimmer, add garlic, gingerroot, and kale ribs, and sauté for 2 minutes. Add kale leaves, 2 tablespoons (28 ml) of water, lemon zest, and ponzu sauce. Simmer covered (leaving a small steam vent) on medium-low until tender, about 8 minutes stirring occasionally and adding broth gradually as needed.

 GO GREEN

Kale is a hardy cold-weather plant in peak season December through February, making it a good option when your other favorite produce is out of season.

 TOTAL PREP AND COOK TIME: 15 MINUTES • YIELD: 5 SERVINGS, ½ CUP (65 G) EACH

PER SERVING: 55 CALORIES; 3 G TOTAL FAT; TRACE SATURATED FAT; 2 G PROTEIN; 6 G CARBOHYDRATE; 2 G DIETARY FIBER; 0 MG CHOLESTEROL.

SUPER SIMPLE SUMMER SQUASH SAUTÉ ▶

This recipe is ridiculously simple, yet delivers a burst of flavor. You can slice the vegetables into half-moons instead of dicing them, if you prefer. Adjust the cooking time as needed.

1 tablespoon (15 ml) extra-virgin olive oil
1½ teaspoons (2 g) dried onion flakes
1 teaspoon (3 g) minced garlic
2 medium zucchini, diced into ½-inch (1.3 cm) cubes (about 2½ cups, or 300 g)
2 medium yellow summer squash, diced into ½-inch (1.3 cm) cubes (about 2½ cups, or 300 g)
¼ teaspoon salt
¼ teaspoon freshly ground black pepper

Heat a large frying pan over medium-low heat and pour in the oil. Sprinkle in the onion flakes and garlic and cook for 15 seconds until aromatic. Add the remaining ingredients and sauté until vegetables are tender, stirring occasionally, about 8 to 10 minutes.

 TOTAL PREP AND COOK TIME: 15 MINUTES • YIELD: 6 SERVINGS, ¾ CUP (APPROX. 100 G) EACH

PER SERVING: 45 CALORIES; 2 G TOTAL FAT; TRACE SATURATED FAT; 1 G PROTEIN; 5 G CARBOHYDRATE; 2 G DIETARY FIBER; 0 MG CHOLESTEROL.

ROASTED CORN OFF THE COB WITH CHILE-LIME SAUCE & MEXICAN CHEESE

I enjoyed this dish for the first time at a Mexican restaurant and quickly decided it was my main dish. The tacos became an afterthought.

FOR CORN:
4 ears of corn, husks and silks removed
2 teaspoons (10 ml) expeller-pressed grapeseed or canola oil
⅛ teaspoon salt
⅛ teaspoon freshly ground black pepper

FOR AIOLI:
¼ cup (60 g) light mayonnaise
1 tablespoon (15 ml) low-fat milk
1 teaspoon (5 ml) lime juice
1 pinch chili powder
1 pinch garlic powder

FOR SERVING:
3 tablespoons (28 g) crumbly Mexican-style cheese, such as queso fresco or cotija (or feta)

Preheat oven to 450°F (230°C, or gas mark 8) and line a sheet pan with parchment paper or a silicone baking mat.

TO MAKE THE CORN: Brush the corn with the oil and sprinkle with salt and pepper. Bake until blistered, about 15 minutes, turning halfway through cooking. Cool slightly. Stand the cobs on a cutting board and holding the cobs firmly, cut off the kernels.

TO MAKE THE AIOLI: Stir the sauce ingredients together in a small bowl.

TO SERVE: Place the corn in serving dishes, drizzle with aioli, and sprinkle on the cheese.

 TOTAL PREP AND COOK TIME: 25 MINUTES • YIELD: 4 SERVINGS, ½ CUP CORN (74.5 G) EACH (WITH 1 TABLESPOON [15 G] AIOLI AND 2 TEASPOONS [6 G] CHEESE)

PER SERVING: 168 CALORIES; 9 G TOTAL FAT; 1 G SATURATED FAT; 4 G PROTEIN; 20 G CARBOHYDRATE; 2 G DIETARY FIBER; 12 MG CHOLESTEROL.

OVEN ROASTED CARROTS & PARSNIPS WITH THYME & NUTMEG

Parsnips (which look like white carrots) tend to get a bad rap, but I think that's because people are simply unfamiliar with this root vegetable. When roasted, they develop a rich, sweet taste that is so comforting during the cold months. Peel and trim them like you would carrots before cutting into desired shapes.

3 carrots, cut into ¾-inch (2 cm) chunks
2 medium parsnips, cut into ¾-inch (2 cm) chunks
1 tablespoon (15 ml) expeller-pressed grapeseed or canola oil
½ teaspoon dried thyme
½ teaspoon ground nutmeg (whole nutmeg, freshly grated, preferred)
¼ teaspoon freshly ground black pepper
⅛ teaspoon salt

Preheat oven to 450°F (230°F, or gas mark 8) and line a large sheet pan with parchment paper or a silicone baking mat. Place the vegetables on the pan, sprinkle on the remaining ingredients, and toss with your hands. Spread the vegetables out in a single layer and bake on the bottom rack until golden, about 35 minutes, turning the vegetables and rotating the pan after 20 minutes. Serve hot.

 GO GREEN

Parsnips require cold weather for optimal development and in the United States are usually harvested from October through December, with some being left in the ground for an early spring harvest. It's best to enjoy them during cold-weather months since they typically are stored in warehouses for the remainder of the year.

TOTAL PREP AND COOK TIME: 45 MINUTES • YIELD: 5 SERVINGS, ½ CUP (APPROX. 77 G) EACH

PER SERVING: 66 CALORIES; 3 G TOTAL FAT; TRACE SATURATED FAT; 1 G PROTEIN; 10 G CARBOHYDRATE; 3 G DIETARY FIBER; 0 MG CHOLESTEROL.

FOOL-THE-FAMILY CAULIFLOWER MASHED POTATOES

I have served this dish to many people who loved it and had no idea it contained cauliflower.

1 large russet potato, peeled
4 cups (400 g) cauliflower florets (about 1 small head)
2 garlic cloves, peeled
½ cup (115 g) nonfat plain Greek yogurt, room temperature
¼ cup (60 ml) organic or reduced sodium vegetable broth, hot
1 tablespoon (14 g) butter
¼ teaspoon + ⅛ teaspoon salt
1 pinch ground nutmeg
1 pinch freshly ground white pepper (or ⅛ teaspoon black pepper)

Cut the potato into approximately 1-inch (2.5 cm) chunks; to prevent browning, immediately put them into a medium pot containing enough cold water to cover them. Add cauliflower, garlic, and more water to cover the vegetables completely. Bring to a boil on high and cook for 8 minutes until fork-tender, reducing heat as needed. Drain thoroughly and mash until smooth and stir in the broth, butter, salt, nutmeg, and pepper. Stir in yogurt.

 RECIPE NOTE

Alternatively, you can purée all the ingredients in a large food processor just until smooth, being careful not to overprocess, which can make the potatoes gluey.

 TOTAL PREP AND COOK TIME: 25 MINUTES •
<30 YIELD: 8 SERVINGS, ½ CUP (APPROX. 98 G) EACH

PER SERVING: 47 CALORIES; 2 G TOTAL FAT; 1 G SATURATED FAT; 2 G PROTEIN; 6 G CARBOHYDRATE; 1 G DIETARY FIBER; 5 MG CHOLESTEROL.

◄ ROASTED CITRUS ASPARAGUS

My friend Meghan has a husband who did not like any vegetables except potatoes and onions until he tasted this dish and loved it. You can also grill the asparagus instead.

1 bunch asparagus, woody bottom third
   cut off
1 teaspoon (2 g) grated orange zest
1 teaspoon (2 g) grated lime zest
1 teaspoon (5 ml) lime juice
⅛ teaspoon salt
⅛ teaspoon freshly ground black pepper
2 teaspoons (10 ml) extra-virgin olive oil

Preheat oven to 450°F (230°C, or gas mark 8) and line a large sheet pan with parchment paper or a silicone baking mat. Arrange asparagus in a single layer on the pan. In a small bowl, whisk together orange and lime zests, lime juice, salt, and pepper and then drizzle in the oil while whisking. Pour evenly over the asparagus. Toss the asparagus gently with your hands to coat completely. Bake 14 minutes until fork-tender.

 TOTAL PREP AND COOK TIME: 20 MINUTES • YIELD: 4 SERVINGS, ABOUT 6 SPEARS EACH

PER SERVING: 29 CALORIES; 2 G TOTAL FAT; TRACE SATURATED FAT; 1 G PROTEIN; 2 G CARBOHYDRATE; 1 G DIETARY FIBER; 0 MG CHOLESTEROL.

BROCCOLI PARMESAN

Broccoli is one of the most nutritious foods you can eat, brimming with vitamin C, folate, fiber, potassium, and disease-fighting phytochemicals. But try explaining that to your kids! Instead, tempt them by smothering broccoli with a favorite pizza sauce.

Expeller-pressed canola oil spray
1 large egg white
1 tablespoon (15 ml) low-fat milk
⅔ cup (77 g) whole-wheat bread crumbs
2 tablespoons (10 g) grated Parmesan
   cheese
½ teaspoon garlic powder
½ teaspoon Italian herb seasoning
⅛ teaspoon salt
⅛ teaspoon freshly ground black pepper
4 cups (284 g) 1½-inch (3.8 cm)-long,
   bite-size broccoli florets
½ cup (125 g) marinara sauce
⅓ cup (38 g) shredded part-skim
   mozzarella cheese

Place 1 oven rack on the second highest level in the oven, 6 inches (15 cm) under the heating element; place another rack in the middle. Preheat oven to 400°F (200°C, or gas mark 6) and coat a 9 x 9-inch (23 x 23 cm) baking pan with canola oil spray.

Beat egg white in a medium bowl and blend in the milk. In another medium bowl, stir together the bread crumbs, Parmesan cheese, garlic powder, Italian seasoning, salt, and pepper. Add broccoli to the egg white, coat well, and then use your hands to toss the broccoli in the bread crumbs.

Arrange broccoli in the pan in an even layer, stems down. Bake on middle rack until lightly golden, about 15 minutes. Remove pan and change the oven setting to high broil. Drizzle marinara sauce on top of broccoli and sprinkle with mozzarella. Place pan on the higher rack and broil until cheese becomes medium golden, about 5 minutes. Enjoy immediately.

 TOTAL PREP AND COOK TIME: 30 MINUTES • YIELD: 6 SERVINGS, ¾ CUP (APPROX. 89 G) EACH

PER SERVING: 137 CALORIES; 3 G TOTAL FAT; 1 G SATURATED FAT; 7 G PROTEIN; 21 G CARBOHYDRATE; 5 G DIETARY FIBER; 7 MG CHOLESTEROL.

CINNAMON RICOTTA SWEET POTATOES

This dish just screams "holidays," but is simple enough to make anytime you have a hankering for candied sweet potatoes. September through November is peak season.

2 medium orange-fleshed sweet potatoes
½ cup (125 g) part-skim ricotta cheese, room temperature
1 tablespoon (20 g) real maple syrup
¼ teaspoon cinnamon
⅛ teaspoon freshly ground black pepper

Preheat oven to 400°F (200°C, or gas mark 6). Pierce each potato a few times with a fork, place on a sheet pan, and bake until fork-tender in the thickest part, about 45 minutes. Cool just until you can handle them. Cut potatoes in half horizontally and scoop flesh into a medium bowl, discarding skins. Mash the potatoes until smooth or purée in a food processor for a smoother consistency. Fold in the ricotta, maple syrup, cinnamon, and pepper and enjoy hot, microwaving to reheat, if needed.

TOTAL PREP AND COOK TIME: 60 MINUTES • YIELD: 8 SERVINGS, ½ CUP (112.5 G) EACH

PER SERVING: 93 CALORIES; 1 G TOTAL FAT; 1 G SATURATED FAT; 3 G PROTEIN; 18 G CARBOHYDRATE; 2 G DIETARY FIBER; 5 MG CHOLESTEROL.

 RECIPE NOTE

Use up leftover ricotta in this mini recipe for Chocolate Ricotta Crème: Mix 1 cup (250 g) ricotta with 1 tablespoon (20 g) honey, 2 teaspoons (3 g) unsweetened cocoa powder, and ¼ teaspoon vanilla.

CHAPTER 7

SECRETLY SKINNY SWEET TREATS

FOUR SEASONS FRUIT PIZZA

Kim was embarrassed to admit her son's manners after he ate this and then licked the plate clean. Scarlet devours this for breakfast.

FOR CRUST:

Expeller-pressed canola oil spray

¼ cup (60 ml) expeller-pressed grapeseed or canola oil

1½ cups (300 g) granulated raw sugar (evaporated cane juice)

2 tablespoons (28 ml) low-fat milk

1 tablespoon (15 ml) vanilla extract

3 large eggs

1 cup (120 g) whole-wheat or white whole-wheat flour

1 cup (125 g) unbleached all-purpose flour, plus extra for dusting

1 tablespoon (14 g) baking powder

¼ teaspoon salt

FOR FILLING:

1 (14-ounce, or 425 ml) can coconut milk (regular, not light), chilled until solid, not shaken

4 ounces (115 g) light cream cheese, slightly softened

2 tablespoons (26 g) granulated raw sugar (evaporated cane juice)

FOR TOPPING:

6 cups (900 g) fruit*

TOTAL PREP AND COOK TIME: 45 MINUTES •
YIELD: 28 SERVINGS, 1 SQUARE EACH

PER SERVING: 155 CALORIES; 7 G TOTAL FAT;
3 G SATURATED FAT; 3 G PROTEIN; 22 G CARBOHY-
DRATE; 2 G DIETARY FIBER; 29 MG CHOLESTEROL.

Preheat oven to 375°F (190°C, or gas mark 5). Coat medium sheet pan with canola oil spray and dust with flour.

TO MAKE THE CRUST: In a medium bowl, whisk oil, sugar, milk, and vanilla and then beat in the eggs one at a time. Add flours, baking powder, and salt and stir just until combined. Do not overmix. Pour evenly into pan and spread with rubber spatula to completely cover the bottom of the pan. Bake until golden, about 15 minutes. Cool completely and then loosen crust from bottom of pan with spatula. Quickly but carefully transfer the pizza to a platter and then decorate with filling and fruit.

TO MAKE THE FILLING: Using a fork, lift the solid portion of the coconut milk out of the can and place it in a chilled, medium-size bowl. Add cream cheese and beat with a hand mixer on high until mixture is smooth and soft peaks form, about 4 minutes. Beat in the sugar. Spread the filling onto the crust, leaving ¼ inch (6 mm) around the edges.

FOR THE TOPPING: Arrange the fruit on top of the crust in a diagonal or concentric pattern. You can also cut into squares first and then decorate with fruit. Refrigerate until ready to serve, or up to 2 days.

 GO GREEN

*You can vary the fruit based around the season.

» **Spring and Summer:** whole blueberries, raspberries, and blackberries; sliced strawberries, mangos, peaches, and nectarines; pitted cherries

» **Fall:** halved grapes; sliced pears and sweet apples dipped in diluted lemon juice (to prevent browning) and pineapple; pomegranate seeds

» **Winter:** sliced kiwi, dried figs, sweet oranges, bananas dipped in diluted lemon juice, and persimmons (ripened in a paper bag on the counter for 2 weeks until translucent and almost liquid)

DARK CHOCOLATE WHOLE-WHEAT BROWNIES

Admittedly, my favorite brownies come from the box of mix I grew up on. But I can do without the hydrogenated oils, artificial flavors, and chemicals. My new and improved recipe fits the bill perfectly with whole grains, nutritious oil, and unrefined sugar. Scarlet calls these brownies "cake," as she does most desserts, and devoured 2 pieces within minutes.

⅓ cup (29 g) unsweetened cocoa powder

½ cup (120 ml) boiling water or coffee

⅓ cup (58 g) dark chocolate chips

½ cup (120 ml) expeller-pressed grape-seed or canola oil

2 teaspoons (10 ml) vanilla extract

3 large eggs, room temperature

1½ cups (150 g) granulated raw sugar (evaporated cane juice)

1 cup (125 g) unbleached all-purpose flour

¾ cup (90 g) whole-wheat flour, plus extra for dusting

¾ teaspoon salt

Preheat oven to 325°F (170°C, or gas mark 3) and grease and lightly flour the bottom only of a 13 x 9-inch (33 x 23 cm) pan. In a large bowl, whisk cocoa powder with boiling liquid until dissolved. Add chocolate chips and stir until melted. Stir in oil and vanilla. In a separate bowl, beat the eggs until frothy and whisk in the sugar. Add to the chocolate. Add the flours and salt at once and fold in just until moistened. Pour batter evenly into the pan and bake on the bottom rack until a toothpick inserted 2 inches (5 cm) from the side of the pan comes out clean or slightly moist, about 30 minutes. Cool completely before cutting into 20 brownies. Store in an airtight container for up to 5 days.

TOTAL PREP AND COOK TIME: 45 MINUTES • YIELD: 20 BROWNIES, 1 EACH

PER SERVING: 170 CALORIES; 8 G TOTAL FAT; 1 G SATURATED FAT; 3 G PROTEIN; 25 G CARBOHYDRATE; 1 G DIETARY FIBER; 28 MG CHOLESTEROL.

MOIST, ONE-BOWL CHOCOLATE CAKE

My neighbor tasted this cake and told me I should be arrested for making a dessert this good. This recipe is very quick and simple. Although I substitute a few cleaner ingredients, the basic cake formula is derived from Mollie Katzen's Six-Minute Chocolate Cake from her wonderful cookbook, *Moosewood Classics*.

Expeller-pressed canola oil spray

FOR CAKE:

1 cup (125 g) unbleached all-purpose flour

½ cup (60 g) chickpea flour (or whole-wheat pastry flour)

1 cup (200 g) granulated raw sugar (evaporated cane juice)

⅓ cup (29 g) unsweetened cocoa powder

1 teaspoon (5 g) baking soda

½ teaspoon salt

1 cup (235 ml) cool water or coffee

½ cup (120 ml) expeller-pressed grape-seed or canola oil

2 teaspoons (10 ml) vanilla extract

2 tablespoons (28 ml) cider vinegar

FOR FROSTING (OPTIONAL):

½ cup (88 g) dark chocolate chips

3 tablespoons (48 g) natural creamy peanut butter

1 tablespoon (15 ml) low-fat milk, warm

1 teaspoon (5 ml) vanilla extract

Preheat oven to 375°F (190°C, or gas mark 5) and coat a 9 x 9-inch (23 x 23 cm) pan with canola oil spray.

TO MAKE THE CAKE: Sift flours, sugar, cocoa powder, baking soda, and salt into a medium bowl. Mix water, oil, and vanilla in a measuring cup and add to the dry ingredients. Whisk until smooth. Swirl in the cider vinegar, stirring quickly until pale stripes are evenly distributed, and pour into the pan. Bake until the cake pulls away from the sides of the pan and springs back in the center when pressed lightly with your fingertip, about 25 to 30 minutes.

TO MAKE THE FROSTING: Microwave the chocolate chips in a bowl, stirring every 30 seconds until smooth. Remove from microwave and stir in the peanut butter and milk and whisk until completely smooth. Spread over cooled cake.

Cut into 12 pieces.

 GO CLEAN

Make a conscious decision to purchase fair trade certified cocoa, which indicates that the farmers and workers in developing nations (where most cocoa is grown) got a better price, safer work conditions, and community resources. This limits the exploitation of these workers and is a more socially and environmentally responsible choice.

TOTAL PREP AND COOK TIME: 45 MINUTES, PLUS COOLING • YIELD: 12 SERVINGS, 1 PIECE EACH

PER SERVING: 280 CALORIES; 15 G TOTAL FAT; 3 G SATURATED FAT; 4 G PROTEIN; 35 G CARBOHYDRATE; 3 G DIETARY FIBER; 0 MG CHOLESTEROL.

PEANUT BRITTLE COOKIE BARS WITH DARK CHOCOLATE DRIZZLE

Part candy, part cookie, these bars are so delicious you won't want to eat just one. You can play around with other nuts in this recipe, such as almonds, pistachios, and pecans.

Expeller-pressed canola oil spray

FOR CRUST:

1¼ cups (105 g) fine whole-grain graham cracker crumbs (about 12 squares)

3 tablespoons (45 ml) expeller-pressed grapeseed or canola oil

2 tablespoons (40 g) honey

FOR FILLING:

⅓ cup (115 g) honey

¼ cup (60 g) packed light brown sugar

⅛ teaspoon salt

3 tablespoons (42 g) cold butter, cut into pieces

1 tablespoon (15 ml) coconut milk or heavy whipping cream

2 cups (290 g) unsalted dry roasted peanuts

FOR CHOCOLATE DRIZZLE:

⅓ cup (58 g) dark or semisweet chocolate chips

Preheat oven to 350ºF (180ºC, or gas mark 4) and generously coat a 9 x 9-inch (23 x 23 cm) baking pan with canola oil spray.

TO MAKE THE CRUST: Whir the graham crackers in a food processor until they are the consistency of fine crumbs and with the motor running, drizzle in the oil and honey. Spread mixture evenly into the bottom of the pan and press it firmly with your hands. Bake for 12 minutes until fragrant and surface appears dry. Cool for at least a few minutes.

TO MAKE THE FILLING: Increase oven temperature to 375ºF (190ºC, or gas mark 5). Bring honey, sugar, and salt to a boil in a medium pot over medium heat, stirring until sugar dissolves, and then boil for 2 minutes without stirring. Add butter and coconut milk and boil for 1 minute, stirring. Remove from heat and fold in the peanuts, coating them completely. Spread peanuts evenly over the crust and bake until bubbly and golden, about 16 minutes. Cool completely.

TO MAKE THE CHOCOLATE DRIZZLE: Microwave the chocolate chips in a bowl, stirring every 30 seconds until smooth. Dip a fork into the chocolate and with a flick of your wrist, splatter the chocolate over the peanuts in a diagonal pattern. Cool and cut into 16 rectangular or diamond shaped bars.

 GO CLEAN

The darker the chocolate, the higher the percentage of cocoa, which means more antioxidant-rich polyphenols. Also, dark chocolate usually contains less added sugar.

TOTAL PREP AND COOK TIME: 35 MINUTES, PLUS COOLING • YIELD: 16 BARS, 1 EACH

PER SERVING: 240 CALORIES; 16 G TOTAL FAT; 4 G SATURATED FAT; 5 G PROTEIN; 22 G CARBOHYDRATE; 2 G DIETARY FIBER; 6 MG CHOLESTEROL.

OATMEAL & CHERRY BREAKFAST COOKIES WITH ALMONDS

These fruit- and fiber-packed cookies are great for on-the-go mornings paired with a glass of milk, latte, or yogurt.

3 cups (240 g) dry old-fashioned or thick-cut oats

1 cup (120 g) white whole-wheat flour (or regular whole-wheat flour)

2 teaspoons (5 g) ground cinnamon

½ teaspoon baking soda

1 large egg

⅓ cup (80 ml) expeller-pressed grapeseed or canola oil

1 cup (225 g) packed light brown sugar

¼ cup (60 ml) low-fat milk

1 teaspoon (5 ml) almond extract (or vanilla extract)

½ cup (80 g) dried tart cherries

½ cup (46 g) sliced almonds, divided

Preheat oven to 350°F (180°C, or gas mark 4) and line 2 large sheet pans with parchment paper or silicone baking mats. Stir oats, flour, cinnamon, and baking soda in a medium bowl. In a large bowl, beat egg and whisk in the oil, sugar, milk, and almond extract. Add the dry ingredients to the wet ingredients and stir just until moistened, adding cherries and half of the almonds toward the end of mixing. Drop scant ¼-cup (55 g) scoops of dough onto the pans at least 2 inches (5 cm) apart, sprinkle remaining almonds on top, and pat gently with waxed paper to flatten slightly. Bake until golden around the edges and set in the middle, about 16 minutes. Cool completely and store in an airtight container for up to 1 week, or freeze for up to 1 month.

 RECIPE NOTE

Feel free to play around with different types of fruits and nuts, such as chopped walnuts, pistachios, or pecans; or raisins and chopped dried apricots. Adding ⅓ cup (58 g) of mini chocolate chips is fun, too.

 TOTAL PREP AND COOK TIME: 40 MINUTES • YIELD: 16 COOKIES, 1 EACH

PER SERVING: 276 CALORIES; 9 G TOTAL FAT; 1 G SATURATED FAT; 7 G PROTEIN; 42 G CARBOHYDRATE; 5 G DIETARY FIBER; 12 MG CHOLESTEROL.

ALMOND BUTTER OATMEAL CHOCOLATE CHIP COOKIES

This may very well become your new go-to chocolate chip cookie recipe. Brimming with oats, whole-wheat flour, and flaxseeds, these cookies can even be enjoyed for breakfast on occasion!

3 tablespoons (21 g) flaxseed meal

1 (4-ounce, or 115 g) stick butter, sliced

1 cup (225 g) packed light brown sugar, clumps broken up

½ cup (100 g) granulated raw sugar (evaporated cane juice)

1 teaspoon (5 ml) pure vanilla extract

1½ cups (390 g) unsweetened almond butter

1¼ cups (156 g) unbleached all-purpose flour

1 cup (120 g) whole-wheat flour

1½ teaspoons (7 g) baking powder

½ teaspoon baking soda

½ teaspoon salt

1¾ cups (140 g) dry oats

1½ cups (263 g) dark chocolate chips

Preheat oven to 375°F (190°C, or gas mark 5) and line 2 large sheet pans with parchment paper or silicone baking mats. In a small bowl, stir together flaxseed meal and ½ cup (120 ml) of water. In an electric mixer fitted with a paddle, beat butter, sugars, and vanilla on medium speed until smooth and slightly fluffy, about 3 minutes. Add flaxseed slurry, almond butter, and ¼ cup (60 ml) of water and beat on low until incorporated. Turn off the mixer, scrape down the sides of the bowl, and add flours, baking powder, baking soda, and salt. Mix on low speed, stopping just before all the ingredients are completely incorporated. Scrape down the sides of the bowl. Add oats and chocolate chips and mix on low just until distributed evenly.

Using a spring handle ice cream scoop or your hands, portion dough into balls of about 2 tablespoons (28 g) each. Place on sheet pans about 1½ inches (3.8 cm) apart. You will need to bake the dough in 2 batches. Slightly flatten each cookie with a fork in a crisscross shape. Bake until lightly golden, about 8 minutes. Cool and store in airtight containers for up to 5 days, or freeze for up to 4 months.

 RECIPE NOTE

Flaxseeds replace the eggs in this recipe, resulting in a more plant-based cookie. You can replace the eggs in other baked goods and breadings with 1 tablespoon (7 g) of ground flaxseeds mixed with 3 tablespoons (45 ml) of water per egg. Allow the flaxseeds to absorb most of the water for a few minutes before incorporating the slurry into recipes. Your body will better absorb essential omega-3 alpha-linolenic acid from flaxseed meal than from whole flaxseeds, which pass through the digestive tract mostly intact.

TOTAL PREP AND COOK TIME: 40 MINUTES • YIELD: 33 COOKIES, 1 EACH

PER SERVING: 238 CALORIES; 14 G TOTAL FAT; 5 G SATURATED FAT; 5 G PROTEIN; 26 G CARBOHYDRATE; 3 G DIETARY FIBER; 7 MG CHOLESTEROL.

CHOCOLATE HAZELNUT BUTTER CRISPY RICE TREATS

On occasion I love a good crispy rice treat made the old-fashioned way, with marshmallows and butter, but I feel better about this recipe in that it is free of artificial food coloring and refined sugars found in packaged marshmallows. These treats take on a whole new flavor profile and taste decadently delicious.

Expeller-pressed canola oil spray

2 tablespoons (14 g) flaxseed meal

½ cup (85 g) raisins

⅓ cup (85 g) natural chocolate hazelnut butter

⅓ cup (107 g) light agave nectar, warm

1 teaspoon vanilla extract

¼ teaspoon salt

½ cup (43 g) unsweetened cocoa powder

4 cups (40 g) brown rice crispy cereal

Coat a 9 x 9-inch (23 x 23 cm) pan with canola oil spray. In a large bowl, stir together the flaxseed meal and 2 tablespoons (28 ml) of water. Place raisins, hazelnut butter, agave nectar, vanilla, and salt in a food processor and whir until it forms a mostly smooth paste. Add to the flaxseed slurry, along with the cocoa powder. Stir in the cereal and immediately pour mixture into the pan, using your hands to pack the mixture into an even surface. Let rest at least 30 minutes, if possible, to allow the bars to firm up before cutting. Wrap tightly or place in an airtight container and store for up to 5 days.

 RECIPE NOTE

Find brown rice crispy cereal in the natural food section. Since some of these cereals are presweetened, you may want to reduce the amount of agave nectar in the recipe.

 GO CLEAN

» Opt for raw or non-Dutched cocoa, which retains more disease-fighting polyphenols and flavanols than alkalized varieties.

» While some chocolate hazelnut butter brands market themselves as healthy, wholesome, and something appropriate for slathering on breakfast foods, the ingredient list may tell another story. Look for those with hazelnuts listed before sugar and palm oil in the ingredients list, which means you're getting more of the good stuff.

 TOTAL PREP AND COOK TIME: 15 MINUTES, PLUS RESTING •
YIELD: 16 TREATS, 1 EACH

PER SERVING: 108 CALORIES; 2 G TOTAL FAT; TRACE SATURATED FAT; 2 G PROTEIN; 22 G CARBOHYDRATE; 2 G DIETARY FIBER; 0 MG CHOLESTEROL.

SNEAKY BEET CHOCOLATE CUPCAKES WITH SWEET CREAM

Your family won't know unless you tell them that these treats are made with whole grains, nutritious oils . . . and beets!

FOR CUPCAKES:

1 (15-ounce, or 425 g) can whole beets (not pickled)

1½ cups (168 g) cake flour (or substitute 1¼ cups minus 1½ teaspoons [144 g] unbleached all-purpose flour)

1 cup (120 g) whole-wheat pastry flour (found in the natural food section)

¼ cup (21 g) unsweetened cocoa powder

¼ teaspoon salt

1½ cups (300 g) granulated raw sugar (evaporated cane juice)

1½ cups (355 ml) expeller-pressed canola or corn oil

2 teaspoons (10 ml) vanilla extract

2 large eggs, room temperature

1½ teaspoons (7 g) baking soda

2 teaspoons (10 ml) white distilled vinegar

FOR FROSTING:

6 ounces (170 g) light cream cheese, slightly softened

¼ cup (55 g) unsalted butter, slightly softened

¼ cup (50 g) granulated raw sugar (evaporated cane juice)

1 teaspoon (5 ml) vanilla extract

3 tablespoons (23 g) dried cranberries, chopped

TO MAKE THE CUPCAKES: Drain beet juice into a small saucepan and simmer over medium-high heat to reduce by nearly half, about 10 minutes. Purée the beets and juice in a blender until smooth.

Preheat oven to 350°F (180°C, or gas mark 4). Line standard muffin tins with paper liners. Sift flours, cocoa powder, and salt into a medium bowl. In a large bowl, beat sugar, oil, and vanilla with a hand mixer. Beat eggs in one at a time until incorporated and then beat on medium-high speed for 3 minutes. Scrape the sides of the bowl. In alternate additions, add ¼ of the flour mixture, then blend on low, and then add ¼ of the beet purée and blend on low. Repeat process three more times until all additions have been fully incorporated.

Combine baking soda and vinegar in a cup and add to the batter, beating just until incorporated. Divide batter evenly among the paper cups, using a ¼-cup (60 ml) measure to fill each cup about half full. Bake for 18 to 24 minutes, rotating the tins halfway through the baking time, until a wooden toothpick inserted into the center of one of the cupcakes comes out clean. Cool the cupcakes in the tins.

TO MAKE THE FROSTING: Beat the cream cheese and butter with a hand mixer, working up to high speed, until fluffy, about 5 minutes. Scrape down the sides of the bowl. Add sugar and vanilla and beat for 2 minutes. Chill until ready to use. Frost the cupcakes and sprinkle with chopped cranberries. Refrigerate cupcakes until ready to serve, up to 3 days.

TOTAL PREP AND COOK TIME: 45 MINUTES, PLUS COOLING TIME • YIELD: 24 CUPCAKES, 1 EACH

PER SERVING: 279 CALORIES; 18 G TOTAL FAT; 3 G SATURATED FAT; 3 G PROTEIN; 29 G CARBOHYDRATE; 1 G DIETARY FIBER; 25 MG CHOLESTEROL.

GRANDMA CRUMER'S BANANA SPLIT TORTE

The inspiration for this recipe came from my grandma's archives, sans three sticks of butter (yes, I'm serious). Don't fret if someone in your family isn't a fan of coconut, because the flavor is mild in the final dish.

Expeller-pressed canola oil spray

FOR CRUST:

1¼ cups (105 g) whole-grain graham cracker crumbs (about 12 squares)
3 tablespoons (45 ml) expeller-pressed grapeseed or canola oil
1 tablespoon (20 g) honey

FOR FILLING:

1½ cups (345 g) low-fat vanilla Greek yogurt
1 tablespoon + 1 teaspoon (11 g) corn-starch, divided
2 tablespoons + 1 teaspoon (30 g) granulated raw sugar (evaporated cane juice), divided
1 (14-ounce, or 425 ml) can coconut milk (regular, not light), chilled, not shaken
3 medium just-ripe bananas
1 (14-ounce, or 390 g) can crushed pine-apple in its own juice, drained well
¼ cup (28 g) chopped pecans, toasted (in a 300ºF [150ºC, or gas mark 2] oven for 10 minutes)
¼ cup (40 g) dried tart cherries, chopped, or 1 cup (155 g) fresh sweet cherries

Preheat oven to 350°F (180°C, or gas mark 4) and coat a 9 x 9-inch (23 x 23 cm) pan with the canola oil spray.

TO MAKE THE CRUST: Whir the graham cracker crumbs in a food processor until finely chopped and with the motor running, drizzle in the oil and honey. Spread the mixture evenly into the bottom of the pan and press firmly with your hands. Bake for 12 minutes until fragrant and surface appears dry. Cool completely.

TO MAKE THE FILLING: In a chilled medium bowl, beat the yogurt with a hand mixer on high, or whisk until soft peaks form, about 3 minutes. Add 1 teaspoon (4 g) of cornstarch and 2 tablespoons (26 g) of sugar and beat for 2 minutes. Using a fork, lift the solid portion of the coconut milk from the can and place it into another chilled medium bowl and beat on high until smooth and fluffy, about 4 minutes. Add the remaining cornstarch and sugar, beating until smooth.

Slice the bananas directly over the crust and distribute them evenly. Spread yogurt filling over the bananas; follow this with the pineapple and then the coconut cream. Chill for 3 hours or up to 3 days, sprinkling pecans and cherries on top just before serving, to preserve texture. Cut into 12 pieces.

 RECIPE NOTE

Speed the chilling time of coconut milk by placing the can in the ice bin of your freezer for 45 minutes. You can drink the electrolyte-rich coconut water that is left over after you remove the solid top portion used in the recipe.

 GO GREEN

Use fresh sweet cherries (that are sourced locally or at least domestically) during their summer peak season. Garnish each serving with 1 or 2 whole cherries or cut into halves and remove the pits.

 TOTAL PREP AND COOK TIME: 30 MINUTES, PLUS CHILLING • **YIELD: 12 SERVINGS, 1 PIECE EACH**

PER SERVING: 233 CALORIES; 13 G TOTAL FAT; 6 G SATURATED FAT; 4 G PROTEIN; 27 G CARBOHYDRATE; 2 G DIETARY FIBER; 1 MG CHOLESTEROL.

LEMONY WHOLE-GRAIN BISCUITS WITH STRAWBERRY RASPBERRY SAUCE

This recipe brings back memories of my childhood sitting at my grandma's kitchen table while enjoying this dessert made of raspberries picked from her garden and strawberries from The Little Farmer, a small "you-pick" farm where I grew up.

FOR SHORTCAKES:

¾ cup (90 g) whole-wheat pastry flour

¾ cup (93 g) unbleached all-purpose flour

1 tablespoon (14 g) baking powder

½ teaspoon salt

¾ cup (172 g) cold low-fat lemon yogurt

¼ cup (60 ml) cold low-fat milk, plus extra for brushing

¼ cup + 2 tablespoons (75 g) granulated raw sugar, divided

2 teaspoons (10 ml) vanilla extract

¼ cup (55 g) cold butter, cut into small cubes

3 tablespoons (15 g) dry old-fashioned oats

FOR BERRY TOPPING:

3 cups (510 g) sliced strawberries

1 cup (125 g) raspberries

2 tablespoons (25 g) granulated raw sugar (evaporated cane juice)

Whipped cream or honey Greek yogurt for topping

Preheat oven to 450°F (230°C, or gas mark 8) and line a large sheet pan with parchment paper or a silicone baking mat.

TO MAKE THE SHORTCAKES: Mix flours, baking powder, and salt in a medium bowl. In another bowl, blend yogurt, milk, ¼ cup (50 g) sugar, and vanilla. Add butter to the dry ingredients, tossing it with your hands, and cut it in with a pastry blender or fork or by squeezing the mixture between your thumbs and forefingers until it resembles a blend of flakes, pebbles, and peas. Add the wet ingredients to this mixture and fold just until moistened. Fold dough over and knead a few times in the bowl. Move dough to a lightly floured surface and then roll or pat it until it is ½-inch (1.3 cm)-thick and in the shape of a square or rectangle. Brush dough with milk, sprinkle it with 2 tablespoons (25 g) sugar and oats, and cut into 8 squares with a sharp knife. Place the dough on the pan and bake until golden around the edges, about 12 minutes.

TO MAKE THE BERRY TOPPING: Stir strawberries, raspberries, and sugar together in a bowl.

Spoon berries over warm biscuits and top with a dollop of cream. Refrigerate leftovers for up to 2 days and reheat biscuits in a 350°F (180°C, or gas mark 4) oven until hot.

TOTAL PREP AND COOK TIME: 45 MINUTES • YIELD: 8 SERVINGS, 1 BISCUIT EACH (WITH ½ CUP [75 G] BERRIES)

PER SERVING: 255 CALORIES; 7 G TOTAL FAT; 4 G SATURATED FAT; 6 G PROTEIN; 42 G CARBOHYDRATE; 4 G DIETARY FIBER; 16 MG CHOLESTEROL.

ORANGE VANILLA CHEESECAKE BARS WITH GINGERSNAP CRUST

Nothing beats a piece of well-made cheesecake, except one that tastes just as good with many fewer calories and less saturated fat. Greek yogurt replaces half of the cream cheese and adds beneficial nutrients, too.

Expeller-pressed canola oil spray

FOR CRUST:

2 ¾ cups (126 g) natural gingersnaps (1½ cups fine crumbs)

3 tablespoons (45 ml) expeller-pressed grapeseed or canola oil

⅛ teaspoon salt

FOR FILLING:

1 (8-ounce, or 225 g) package light cream cheese, at room temperature for 30 minutes

1 cup (230 g) nonfat plain Greek yogurt

½ cup (100 g) granulated raw sugar (evaporated cane juice)

3 large eggs

3 tablespoons (23 g) unbleached all-purpose flour

1 large orange, 2 teaspoons (4 g) grated zest and 3 ounces (90 ml) juice

2 tablespoons (28 ml) lemon juice

1 vanilla bean, slit open lengthwise, inside bean paste scraped out (or 2 teaspoons [10 ml] vanilla extract)

Preheat oven to 350°F (180°C, or gas mark 4) and coat a 9 x 9-inch (23 x 23 cm) pan with canola oil spray.

TO MAKE THE CRUST: Whir the gingersnaps in a food processor until they reach the consistency of fine crumbs; with the motor running, drizzle in the oil and sprinkle in the salt and mix until blended completely. Spread crumbs evenly into the pan and ½ inch (1.3 cm) up the sides. Press crumbs firmly. Bake for 11 minutes until fragrant and surface appears dry.

TO MAKE THE FILLING: Beat the cream cheese with a hand mixer or whisk until smooth. Add yogurt and sugar and beat until smooth. Whisk in the eggs one at a time until incorporated completely. Add flour, orange zest and juice, lemon juice, and vanilla bean paste. Pour the filling into the crust and bake for 10 minutes. Reduce heat to 325°F (170°C, or gas mark 3) and bake for an additional 35 minutes until only the center jiggles when shaken gently. Place the pan on a cooling rack and allow it to reach room temperature; then chill for at least 4 hours or up to 3 days. Cut into 16 bars.

 GO CLEAN

Otherwise known as turbinado sugar, evaporated cane juice is made from unrefined, minimally processed sugar cane juice left with trace minerals. While white cane sugar comes from the same juice, it is processed with chemical additives and passed through bone char filters. The process requires vast amounts of cow bones and energy to give sugar its pristine white appearance.

TOTAL PREP AND COOK TIME: 1 HOUR, PLUS CHILLING TIME • YIELD: 16 BARS, 1 EACH

PER SERVING: 138 CALORIES; 7 G TOTAL FAT; 2 G SATURATED FAT; 4 G PROTEIN; 15 G CARBOHYDRATE; 1 G DIETARY FIBER; 50 MG CHOLESTEROL.

BLUEBERRY WHOLE-GRAIN SLUMP

Half cobbler, half cake, this easygoing dessert is perfect with a tall glass of home-brewed iced tea on a lazy summer day.

6 cups (870 g) fresh blueberries
½ cup (160 g) light agave nectar
1 tablespoon (6 g) grated lemon zest
½ teaspoon cinnamon
½ cup (63 g) unbleached all-purpose flour
½ cup (60 g) whole-wheat pastry or white
  whole-wheat flour
¼ cup (60 g) packed light brown sugar
1½ teaspoons (7 g) baking powder
¼ teaspoon salt
½ cup (120 ml) low-fat milk
2 tablespoons (28 g) expeller-pressed
  grapeseed or canola oil
¼ cup (20 g) dry oats
Vanilla Greek yogurt for topping

Preheat oven to 375ºF (190ºC, or gas mark 5). Place blueberries in a 3-quart (2.8 L) casserole dish, deep 9 x 9-inch (23 x 23 cm) pan, or deep-dish pie plate. Drizzle evenly with agave and sprinkle with lemon zest and cinnamon. Stir gently to combine.

In a medium bowl, whisk together flours, sugar, baking powder, and salt. Add milk and oil and stir just until smooth. Drop the batter evenly over the blueberries, spread, and sprinkle dry oats on top.

Place the filled dish on a sheet pan to contain spills and bake on the middle rack until golden in the middle and a toothpick inserted into the middle topping comes out clean, about 40 minutes. Cool for at least 30 minutes before cutting into 16 servings. Serve warm in bowls with a dollop of yogurt.

TOTAL PREP AND COOK TIME: 1 HOUR 10 MINUTES • YIELD: 16 SERVINGS, 1 PIECE EACH

PER SERVING: 221 CALORIES; 4 G TOTAL FAT; TRACE SATURATED FAT; 5 G PROTEIN; 43 G CARBOHYDRATE; 3 G DIETARY FIBER; 1 MG CHOLESTEROL.

 GO GREEN

During cold months, when virtually tasteless berries must travel from other countries, opt instead for 6 cups (930 g) of frozen berries, thawing before adding to the recipe.

PEAR-APPLE GRANOLA CRISP WITH GINGER

This dessert is the ultimate comfort food for a cold fall evening and takes advantage of the abundance of apples and pears available in many parts of the world.

FOR FILLING:

3 Granny Smith apples (or other tart variety), peeled, quartered, cored, sliced crosswise ¼ inch (6 mm)

2 firm pears, peeled, quartered, cored, sliced crosswise ¼ inch (6 mm)

¼ cup (85 g) honey

1 tablespoon (15 ml) lemon juice

1 teaspoon (3 g) grated gingerroot

1 teaspoon (2 g) cinnamon

1 teaspoon (5 ml) vanilla extract

Expeller-pressed canola oil spray

FOR TOPPING:

½ cup (60 g) whole-wheat flour

¼ cup (60 g) light brown sugar

1 pinch salt

3 tablespoons (42 g) cold butter, cut into small cubes

2 cups (250 g) granola with nuts and no dried fruit, large clusters broken up

Honey-flavored Greek yogurt or light vanilla ice cream

Preheat oven to 350°F (180°C, or gas mark 4).

TO MAKE THE FILLING: Place apples and pears in a 9 x 9-inch (23 x 23 cm) pan and sprinkle in the honey, lemon juice, gingerroot, cinnamon, and vanilla. Toss well. Coat the upper sides of the pan with canola oil spray.

TO MAKE THE TOPPING: Stir together flour, sugar, and salt. Add butter and press the mixture between your fingers, breaking up the butter until it is pea-size. Add the granola. Spread the topping evenly over the filling.

Bake* until the top is golden and a fork slides easily into the fruit in the middle of the pan, about 50 minutes. Allow to rest for 10 minutes before cutting into 12 pieces. Top with a dollop of yogurt or ice cream.

 GO CLEAN

Choose granola made with whole grains, such as oats, that are listed first in the ingredients instead of sugar and a saturated fat content of 3 grams or less per serving.

 RECIPE NOTE

*If uncooked ingredients are flush with the top rim of the baking dish, place the dish on a sheet pan to prevent oven spills.

TOTAL PREP AND COOK TIME: 1 HOUR 30 MINUTES • YIELD: 12 SERVINGS, 1 PIECE EACH

PER SERVING: 206 CALORIES; 5 G TOTAL FAT; 2 G SATURATED FAT; 3 G PROTEIN; 40 G CARBOHYDRATE; 3 G DIETARY FIBER; 8 MG CHOLESTEROL.

FOUR-LAYER CARROT CAKE WITH PINEAPPLE FILLING

What a delicious way to get your beta-carotene.

FOR CAKE:

1 cup (120 g) whole-wheat pastry flour

1 cup (125 g) unbleached all-purpose flour

1 teaspoon (5 g) baking powder

1 teaspoon (5 g) baking soda

1 teaspoon (2 g) ground cinnamon

1 teaspoons (2 g) ground ginger

¼ teaspoon ground nutmeg

¼ teaspoon salt

1 cup (225 g) packed light brown sugar

½ cup (120 ml) expeller-pressed grape-seed or canola oil

3 large eggs, room temperature

3 cups (330 g) finely shredded carrots (about 7 medium)

½ cup (75 g) golden raisins, steeped 10 minutes in ¼ cup (60 ml) boiling water, drained

1 cup (235 ml) low-fat milk, room temperature

FOR FROSTING:

1 (14-ounce, or 425 ml)-can coconut milk (regular, not light), chilled, not shaken

1 (8-ounce, or 225 g)-package light cream cheese

¼ cup (50 g) granulated raw sugar (evaporated cane juice)

1 tablespoon (8 g) cornstarch

FOR FILLING:

1 (20-ounce, or 560 g) can crushed pine-apple in its own juice, drained well

½ cup (164 g) prepared frosting (from above)

Preheat oven to 350°F (180°C, or gas mark 4) and grease and flour two 9-inch (23 cm) round cake pans.

TO MAKE THE CAKE: Sift flours, baking powder, baking soda, cinnamon, ginger, nutmeg, and salt into a medium bowl. In a large bowl, beat sugar and oil with a hand mixer. Beat eggs in one at a time, and then beat 5 more minutes on medium-high speed. Add carrots and raisins. Add ⅓ of the dry ingredients to the wet ingredients and stir just until moistened; then stir in ⅓ of the milk. Repeat alternately with flours and milk just until moistened. Pour batter equally into the pans and bake until a toothpick inserted into the center of each cake comes out clean, 25 minutes. Cool in the pans for 10 minutes on wire racks. Run a dinner knife around inside rim to release edges. Hold pan at an angle upside down, with your other hand or wire rack directly underneath. Tap bottom of pan briskly to release the cakes from the pans and set on wire rack. Cool completely.

TO MAKE THE FROSTING: Using a fork, lift the solid portion of the coconut milk out of the can and place it into a chilled medium bowl; then add cream cheese. Beat on high with a hand mixer until smooth and soft peaks form, about 4 minutes. Add sugar and cornstarch and beat until smooth.

TO MAKE THE FILLING: Mix the pineapple and ½ cup (164 g) of the prepared frosting together in a bowl.

Using a long serrated knife carefully cut the cakes in half horizontally to make 4 layers. Place 1 cake layer on a serving plate and spread one-third of the filling over the top; repeat 2 times, ending with the fourth cake layer on top. Spread the top and sides of the cake with frosting and chill until ready to serve, up to 3 days. Slice into wedges.

TOTAL PREP AND COOK TIME: 1 HOUR 10 MINUTES, PLUS COOLING • YIELD: 16 SERVINGS, 1 WEDGE EACH

PER SERVING: 305 CALORIES; 14 G TOTAL FAT; 7 G SATURATED FAT; 5 G PROTEIN; 36 G CARBOHYDRATE; 2 G DIETARY FIBER; 45 MG CHOLESTEROL.

QUICK-FIX TRAIL MIX SNACK BARS

This is a recipe I perfected while working as a private chef. I wrapped and stored the bars individually in the fridge for family members to "grab and go" for snacks between work, school, errands, and activities, and I encourage you to do the same. They're a fraction of the cost of high-quality store-bought bars.

Expeller-pressed canola oil spray
1 cup (140 g) raw cashews
¼ cup (35 g) dried tart cherries (or [35 g] raisins)
1 cup (140 g) toasted pepitas (shelled pumpkin seeds)
½ cup (73 g) raw sunflower seeds
⅓ cup (48 g) raw sesame seeds
3 tablespoons (21 g) flaxseed meal
½ teaspoon salt
¼ cup (85 g) honey
1 teaspoon (5 ml) vanilla extract

Preheat oven to 300°F (150°C, or gas mark 2) and coat a 9 x 9-inch (23 x 23 cm) pan with canola oil spray. Finely chop cashews and dried fruit in a food processor (or smash the nuts in a bag, and chop the fruit) and add to a large bowl. Add pepitas, sunflower and sesame seeds, flaxseed, and salt and stir to combine. In a separate bowl, microwave the honey for a few seconds until warm. Drizzle honey and vanilla into the nut mixture and stir until completely incorporated. Pour the mixture into the pan and spread evenly. Spray a sheet of waxed paper with canola oil spray; place the waxed paper on top of the mixture, spray side down, and pack down gently with your hands. Bake until golden, 20 minutes; cool completely.

Place a cutting board on top of the pan. Lay one of your hands on top of the board and the other hand underneath the pan and firmly flip the pan upside down to release the cake from the pan. Cut into 12 bars. For maximum freshness, store bars individually in snack bags and refrigerate for up to 1 month.

 RECIPE NOTES

» For a treat, mix in mini chocolate chips in place of some or all of the fruit.

» Stirring in 2 tablespoons (32 g) of nut butter adds a pleasant, creamy texture.

» Old-fashioned rolled oats can be substituted for the sesame seeds.

 TOTAL PREP AND COOK TIME: 30 MINUTES, PLUS COOLING • YIELD: 16 SERVINGS, 1 BAR EACH

PER SERVING: 260 CALORIES; 18 G TOTAL FAT; 3 G SATURATED FAT; 10 G PROTEIN; 17 G CARBOHYDRATE; 3 G DIETARY FIBER; 0 MG CHOLESTEROL.

WHOLE-GRAIN PUMPKIN SNACK CAKE WITH CHOCOLATE CHIPS

I love this for breakfast or an afternoon snack. You can freeze halves, quarters, or slices for up to 1 month and enjoy again "fresh" when the craving strikes.

Expeller-pressed canola oil spray

1 cup (120 g) whole-wheat pastry flour (or white whole-wheat flour)

1 cup (125 g) unbleached all-purpose flour, plus additional for dusting

2 teaspoons (9 g) baking powder

2 teaspoons (9 g) baking soda

½ teaspoon ground ginger

¼ teaspoon ground cloves

¼ teaspoon ground nutmeg

½ teaspoon salt

1 (15-ounce, or 425 g) can pure solid-pack pumpkin (not pumpkin pie filling)

1 cup (340 g) honey

¼ cup (60 ml) expeller-pressed grapeseed or canola oil

2 large eggs, room temperature

1 teaspoon (2 g) grated orange zest

½ cup (88 g) dark chocolate chips

⅓ cup (40 g) chopped walnuts (optional)

Preheat oven to 325°F (170°C, or gas mark 3) and spray a 9 x 9-inch (23 x 23 cm) baking pan. Mix flours, baking powder, baking soda, ginger, cloves, nutmeg, and salt in a large mixing bowl. In another bowl, stir together the pumpkin, honey, oil, eggs one at a time, and orange zest. Add the wet ingredients to the dry ingredients and stir until almost moistened. Fold in the chocolate chips and walnuts. Pour into the pan and spead evenly, avoiding overhandling. Bake until a wooden skewer inserted into the center of the bread comes out clean, about 40 minutes. Cool in the pan on a wire rack and cut into 12 slices.

TOTAL PREP AND COOK TIME: 1 HOUR • YIELD: 16 SERVINGS, 1 SLICE EACH

PER SERVING: 290 CALORIES; 11 G TOTAL FAT; 3 G SATURATED FAT; 5 G PROTEIN; 46 G CARBOHYDRATE; 3 G DIETARY FIBER; 35 MG CHOLESTEROL.

 RECIPE NOTE

Alternatively, you can bake the bread in four 5 x 3-inch (13 x 7.5 cm) mini loaf pans for 35 minutes.

LIME BASIL WATERMELON COOLER

Watermelon has 92 percent water content, so it provides a lusciously hydrating boost of fluids for only 40 calories per cup. We can all cheer to that!

1 cup (24 g) basil leaves, branches left intact for easy removal
2 tablespoons (40 g) light agave nectar
7 cups (1 kg) watermelon chunks
¼ cup + 1 tablespoon (75 ml) lime juice

Place basil and agave nectar in a large pitcher and grind together with a muddler or the handle end of a wooden spoon to release the basil flavor. Place half of the watermelon chunks and all the lime juice in a blender and purée until smooth, working up to high speed. Hold a fine strainer over the pitcher and pour in all but about 1 cup (235 ml) of the liquid through the strainer, pressing the juice through the strainer by swirling it with a ladle. Purée the remaining watermelon chunks and strain the liquid into the pitcher. Chill for at least 1 hour, up to 4 days, removing the basil after 1 day. Serve cold over crushed ice.

 GO CLEAN

If you think watermelon is little more than a refreshing summer-time treat, think again. Water-melon boasts more lycopene (an antioxidant) than any other fresh fruit or vegetable, is an excellent source of vitamins A and C, and is a good source of vitamin B6.

 RECIPE NOTES

» If you don't have a fine strainer to catch the seeds, be sure to use seedless watermelon.

» You can enjoy this drink immediately by prechilling the pitcher and watermelon before mixing.

» For adults only, try stirring 1½ ounces (42 ml) of tequila into each serving. Garnish with a lime wedge.

 TOTAL PREP AND COOK TIME: 15 MINUTES, PLUS CHILLING • YIELD: 6 SERVINGS, ¾ CUP (175 ML) EACH

PER SERVING: 71 CALORIES; TRACE TOTAL FAT; TRACE SATURATED FAT; 1 G PROTEIN; 18 G CARBOHYDRATE; 1 G DIETARY FIBER; TRACE CHOLESTEROL.

MINT HIBISCUS LEMONADE

This gorgeous, ruby red tea originates from the leaves of the hibiscus flower, a plant you've probably spotted in lush landscapes or tropical climates such as Mexico or Hawaii. Many coffee shops and tea brands market hibiscus tea under the name "Passion" or "Red Raspberry." Read the label and look for "hibiscus" listed as a main ingredient. The amount of agave nectar used will appeal to most partygoers; however, for light everyday sipping, I prefer a little less sweetener. For a boost, I might even fill half the glass with unsweetened brewed tea. For adults only, try stirring in 1½ ounces (42 ml) of vodka per ¾ cup (175 ml) lemonade.

1 large "Red Raspberry Zinger" tea bag (or 4 small "Passion" tea bags)

5 medium mint sprigs (about 3 inches [7.5 cm] each), plus extra for garnish (optional)

½ cup (120 ml) fresh lemon juice (about 3 lemons)

½ cup (160 g) light agave nectar

In a saucepan over high heat, bring 4 cups (1 L) of water to a boil. Place tea bag and mint in a heatproof glass pitcher or bowl. Once the water begins to boil, remove from heat and allow to rest 1 minute so as not to damage the tea leaves. Pour the water into the pitcher and steep for 10 to 15 minutes, covered. Discard tea bag and mint. Stir in the agave nectar until dissolved and add lemon juice. Cool the tea until it nears room temperature and chill for 1 hour, up to 5 days. For a more refined, clarified version, you can strain the tea through a fine sieve or coffee filter before serving cold over crushed ice.

 GO CLEAN

Research shows that hibiscus is high in antioxidants, including vitamin C and anthocyanins. Animal studies indicate that it may be helpful in lowering cholesterol, blood pressure, fever, and pain.

 RECIPE NOTE

If you're craving a Mexican-themed meal, this recipe easily transitions into that flavor profile by substituting lime juice for lemon. You can use tequila instead of vodka and add a splash of triple sec if you're feeling feisty!

 TOTAL PREP AND COOK TIME: 15 MINUTES, PLUS CHILLING • YIELD: 6 SERVINGS, AMPLE ¾ CUP (175 ML) EACH

PER SERVING: 87 CALORIES; 0 G TOTAL FAT; 0 G SATURATED FAT; TRACE PROTEIN; 24 G CARBOHYDRATE; TRACE DIETARY FIBER; 0 MG CHOLESTEROL.

GREEN TEA FRUIT PUNCH

Serve this poolside or at a ladies' lunch or make a decaffeinated version for a kids' party. You can easily change the flavor with orange or berry infused tea bags.

6 green tea bags
2½ cups (364 g) assorted fresh fruit, chopped or sliced into bite-size pieces
2 cups (475 ml) 100 percent white grape juice, chilled

In a saucepan over high heat, bring 2 cups (475 ml) of water to a boil. Place tea bags in a heatproof glass pitcher or bowl. Once the water begins to boil, remove it from the heat and allow it to rest for 1 minute to prevent damaging the tea leaves. Pour the water into the pitcher and steep for 2 minutes, covered. Discard the tea bags and add 2 cups room temperature water (475 ml). Cool the tea to room temperature. Add fruit and white grape juice and chill for 1 hour, up to 2 days. Serve over crushed ice.

 GO GREEN

Enjoy the seasons by using fruit that is at its peak.

Spring and Summer: raspberries; sliced strawberries, mangos, peaches, and nectarines

Fall: halved grapes; sliced pears, sweet apples, and pineapple

Winter: sliced kiwi, sweet oranges, tangerines, blood oranges, and grapefruit

 RECIPE NOTE

For a festive addition, substitute sparkling white grape juice or apple cider for still grape juice.

 TOTAL PREP AND COOK TIME: 30 MINUTES • YIELD: 5 SERVINGS, 1½ CUPS (355 ML) EACH

PER SERVING: 122 CALORIES; 0 G TOTAL FAT; 0 G SATURATED FAT; 1 G PROTEIN; 31 G CARBOHYDRATE; 2 G DIETARY FIBER; 0 MG CHOLESTEROL.

RESOURCES

"**Vegetable Production in Alabama.**" Alabama Cooperative Extension System. ACES Publications, n.d. Web. Oct. 2011 to Feb. 2012. <www.aces.edu/pubs/docs/indexes/anrho.php>.

"**Popular seafood: Best and worst choices.**" Environmental Defense Fund. N.d. Web. Oct. 2011 to Feb. 2012. <http://apps.edf.org/page.cfm?tagID=1521>.

Environmental Protection Agency. "**Emission Factor Documentation for AP-42 Section 9.11.1, Vegetable Oil Processing Final Report.**" November 1995. Web. April 2010. <www.epa.gov/ttn/chief/ap42/ch09/bgdocs/b9s11-1.pdf>.

Miller, K.B., et al. "**Impact of alkalization on the antioxidant and flavanol content of commercial cocoa powders.**" *Journal of Agricultural and Food Chemistry*. 2008. Web. Oct. 2011 to Feb. 2012. <www.ncbi.nlm.nih.gov/pubmed/18710243>.

"**Seafood Watch.**" Monterey Bay Aquarium. N.d. Web. Oct. 2011 to Feb. 2012. <www.montereybayaquarium.org/cr/seafoodwatch.aspx>.

"**Crop Profiles and Timelines.**" North Central IPM Center. U.S. Dept. of Agriculture, National Institute of Food and Agriculture. N.d. Web. Oct. 2011 to Feb. 2012. <www.ipmcenters.org/CropProfiles/index.cfm>.

"**Commercial Vegetable Production Guides.**" Oregon State University. April 2005. Web. Oct. 2011 to Feb. 2012. <http://nwrec.hort.oregonstate.edu/vegindex.html>.

Ali, B.H., et al. "**Phytochemical, pharmacological and toxicological aspects of Hibiscus sabdariffa L.: a review.**" *Phytotherapy Research*. May 2005. Web. Jan. 2012. <www.ncbi.nlm.nih.gov/pubmed/16106391>.

"**Study: U.S. seafood import testing inadequate.**" SeafoodSource.com. Nov. 2011. Web. Dec. 2011. <www.seafoodsource.com/newsarticledetail.aspx?id=12890>.

Shadix, Kyle "**Reducing Sodium in Canned Beans — Easier Than 1-2-3.**" *Today's Dietitian*. Jan. 2010. Web. Dec. 2011. <http://todaysdietitian.com/newarchives/011110p62.shtml>.

"**Free Publications.**" University of California Vegetable Research and Information Center. N.d. Web. Oct. 2011 to Feb. 2012. <http://ucanr.org/freepubs/freepubsub.cfm?cat=1>.

"**Commercial Vegetable & Fruit Production.**" University of Minnesota Extension. N.d. Web. Oct. 2011 to Feb. 2012. <www.extension.umn.edu/Vege&Fruit/>.

ACKNOWLEDGMENTS

Much like bringing a child into the world, words cannot truly describe the love, care, and dedication that it's taken to deliver my first cookbook.

While it was my dream to write my own cookbook someday, I didn't quite know where to begin. After meeting my soon-to-be agent Lisa Ekus, my thoughts stirred for a year, over the course of birthing my baby, and shortly afterwards I popped out a book proposal. Lisa and Sally Ekus became my co-agents, helped shape my idea, and believed in me and my book for the long haul.

My proposal piqued the interest of Amanda Waddell, editor at Fair Winds Press. She conceived the perfect title and saw the book through its production. Thanks for pushing me to think outside the box and deliver a book I'm so proud of. Thank you to publisher Will Kiester for your stamp of approval, and Kevin Mulroy for later jumping in as publisher, publicist Dalyn Miller, and project manager Betsy Gammons.

Day in, day out, I wrote and rewrote, tested, and retested recipes. Kim Crichton, my dedicated production assistant—I couldn't have finished this book on time without you. Jeannette Dickey, my copyeditor, thank you for your candidness and for polishing the proposal and drafts; and Audrey Doyle, for editing the final draft with a fine-toothed comb.

To the creative team—art director Heather Godin and Rita Sowins for the book's beautifully clean design, and Stephanie and Duane Green for styling and shooting the delicious photos. Diane Aiello, thank you for being my hair, makeup, and fashion stylist extraordinaire.

Thanks also to friends, family, and acquaintances who tested the recipes and provided feedback: Kimberly Hughes, the Kane family, the Lane family, Lynn Ladd, Meghan Llanes, Simin Levinson, Anita Westlake, Jenn Wilke, Linda Miller, Julie Jewell, Melissa Nystrom, Desirae Jimenez, the Jantz family, Monica Ulmer, Mona Balma, Sandy Rasmussen, and Andrea Simonich.

Thank you Grandma Crumer, for encouraging (no, telling) me to take my first nutrition class which spawned my entire career; and Grandma Richter, for helping me discover our family's Lebanese recipes. Thanks to my mom Bonnie Ward, sister Lauren Monroe, the Dudash family, Brittany McGee, and friends Lisa and Jeff Geyser and Natalie and Tyler Hill for your support. I'm grateful for my professional colleagues Sharon Salomon, Elisa Zied, and Marlene Koch for their priceless nuggets of wisdom, and for my clients who've been with me over these years.

The biggest thanks of all goes to my husband Steve who supports me in everything I do. Thanks for allowing me to disappear until the wee hours while working on my book, watching our daughter Scarlet on weekends, and eating the same recipes for days on end until I perfected it. Scarlet, thank you for understanding "Mommy's working" and being such a good girl. Lastly, Dad, I wish you were here to see my dreams come true.

Last but certainly not least, I am grateful to my fans, many who have become online friends, who are there for me to provide suggestions, ideas, and feedback.

ABOUT THE AUTHOR

Michelle Dudash, R.D., is an award-winning registered dietitian, Cordon Bleu–certified chef, healthy recipe columnist for *The Arizona Republic* and television personality. Her recipes have appeared in Martha Stewart's *Whole Living* and in *Better Homes and Gardens*, and have also been served at A-list celebrity events. She is frequently quoted in publications such as USAToday.com, *Prevention*, MSN.com, *Family Circle*, *Woman's Day*, and *Women's World* and has appeared nationally on FOX and Friends, Better, and Radio Disney.

Michelle has cooked at a Mobil Five Star restaurant and was a private chef serving guests including English royalty. She graduated from the University of Wisconsin-Madison with a B.S. degree in dietetics, and a few years later she earned her toque from Le Cordon Bleu College of Culinary Arts. She lives in Scottsdale, Arizona.

For more recipes and clean eating tips, visit Michelle online at www.michelledudash.com.

INDEX